The YOUTH FLAG FOOTBALL Handbook

Pathways Press

© **Copyright 2025 - All rights reserved.**

The content contained within this book may not be reproduced, duplicated or transmitted without direct written permission from the author or the publisher.

Under no circumstances will any blame or legal responsibility be held against the publisher, or author, for any damages, reparation, or monetary loss due to the information contained within this book, either directly or indirectly.

Legal Notice:

This book is copyright protected. It is only for personal use. You cannot amend, distribute, sell, use, quote or paraphrase any part, or the content within this book, without the consent of the author or publisher.

Disclaimer Notice:

Please note the information contained within this document is for educational and entertainment purposes only. All effort has been executed to present accurate, up to date, reliable, complete information. No warranties of any kind are declared or implied. Readers acknowledge that the author is not engaged in the rendering of legal, financial, medical or professional advice. The content within this book has been derived from various sources. Please consult a licensed professional before attempting any techniques outlined in this book.

By reading this document, the reader agrees that under no circumstances is the author responsible for any losses, direct or indirect, that are incurred as a result of the use of the information contained within this document, including, but not limited to, errors, omissions, or inaccuracies.

TABLE OF CONTENTS

Introduction 1

Chapter 1: Building a Strong Foundation 7
    Origins of Flag Football 9
    Flag Football Definition... 11
    Who Plays and Why It Matters.. 16

Chapter 2: The Big Benefits... 21
    Physical Growth and Coordination.................................... 23

Chapter 3 Navigating League Types,
Gear, and First-Day Essentials 35
    Essential Equipment Checklist for Kids and Coaches 38
    Introducing the Team - First-Day
    Icebreakers and Building Trust 41
    Common Myths and Misconceptions 43

Chapter 4 Mastering Rules - Clarity
and Confidence for Kids and Adults............................ 53
    Youth Flag Football Rules 58

Clarifying the Flow of the Game:
From Kickoff to Final Whistle 61
Penalties, Fouls, and Fair Play 65
Glossary of Kid-Friendly Flag Football Terms 68
Quick-Reference Cheat Sheets for Game Day 73

Chapter 5 Practice Like a Pro- Winning Structure for Every Session 79
Keeping Every Kid Moving:
Rotations, Stations, and Small Groups............................ 86
What to Do When Half the Team Shows Up 90

**Chapter 6: Core Skills:
Drills for Every Age and Ability** 101
Flag Pulling 101 — Techniques,
Games, and Fixes for Common Mistakes 102
Safe Hand-Offs and Lateral Pitches for Young Players ... 112
Drills for Shy or Less Athletic Kids -
Confidence-Building Activities....................................... 118

**Chapter 7: Managing People:
Communication, Parenting, and Team Culture** 123
Clear Communication.. 125
Dealing with Sideline Coaching and
Over-Involved Parents.. 128
Parent Engagement - Simple Ways to
Get Families Involved.. 131
Constructive Feedback - Encouragement
That Builds Confidence 133

Handling Discipline and Disappointment -
Growth-Minded Responses 136
Teamwork, Leadership, and Sportsmanship 139
Handling Upsets, Mistakes, and Disagreements 143

**Chapter 8: Tools, Resources,
and Next-Level Coaching** 149
Tools and Resources for the Modern Coach 151
Digital Diagrams & Visual Playbooks 159
Season-Long Skill Progression Maps by Age Group 169
Milestones, Skill Checks & Coaching Badges 179
Troubleshooting and Triumph 183

Conclusion: Under the Lights 187

References 189

INTRODUCTION

If you've ever tried explaining flag football to someone who's never seen it, you know the look you get, the one that says, "Wait, so you don't tackle each other? Then what's the point?" I've seen that look a hundred times. And honestly, I used to give it myself. Because let's face it, the words "non-contact" and "football" sound like opposites. But give it one Saturday morning, a patch of grass, a handful of kids with too-big jerseys, and a few parents holding coffee cups like life preservers, and you'll understand exactly why this sport matters.

Flag football isn't just "football without the hits." It's football distilled to its essence: teamwork, timing, trust, and joy. It's where kids learn how to communicate without shouting, compete without bruising, and celebrate without leaving anyone behind. And for coaches like me, it's a front-row seat to watch confidence form in real time.

The first time I volunteered to coach, I thought, "How hard can it be? It's just flag football." I showed up with one whistle, a handful of cones, and no idea how to keep 12 six-year-olds focused for longer than 30 seconds. Within 10 minutes, one kid was crying because someone "stole" his flag, another was chasing butterflies, and the rest had formed a circle arguing over who got to be quarterback. Somewhere between the chaos and the laughter, I realized this was less about perfect plays and more about building something bigger.

That season taught me everything I needed to know about why this handbook was needed. Because the truth is, flag football looks simple until you try to teach it. Every new coach, parent, or volunteer quickly discovers there's a gap between enthusiasm and structure. You can Google drills, print random plays, and borrow advice from a YouTube video, but when you're standing in the middle of a field surrounded by excited kids, that patchwork plan unravels fast.

I wrote this handbook to close that gap, to turn confusion into confidence, frustration into fun, and scattered afternoons into smooth, meaningful practices. This isn't a manual written from an ivory tower; it's born from muddy shoes, missed flags, and those moments when everything finally clicks. It's for the coach who's still learning what a "route tree" is, for the parent who just wants to help their kid love the game, and for the volunteer who said "yes" without knowing exactly what they signed up for. It's for the kid who might never play tackle football but still wants to belong to something that feels like a team.

You'll find plenty of guides out there that try to sound official, packed with jargon, rigid schemes, and advice that assumes you already know half the sport. That's not this book. This one is built for real people. For the dad running late from work who's trying to remember which cone drill to set up. For the mom who's reading this on her phone while waiting for practice to start. For the kid who just wants to understand why everyone keeps yelling "pull the flag!"

Flag football has grown into one of the fastest-rising youth sports in the country, and for good reason. It's safe, inclusive, affordable, and most of all, fun. Every child gets a chance to touch the ball, make a play, and hear their name cheered from the sideline. You don't have to be big, fast, or athletic—you just have to show up. In an age where kids spend more time staring at screens than looking up at each other, flag football brings them back outside, back to laughter, and back to community.

But here's the thing: even a great sport can fall flat without the right support. Too often, new coaches feel thrown into the deep end. They love the game but lack structure. Parents want to help but don't know how. Kids want to learn but get lost in drills that don't fit their age or ability. That's why this handbook exists: to make flag football simple, organized, and deeply enjoyable for everyone involved.

When I started outlining this book, I pictured every kind of reader. The enthusiastic volunteer coach juggling work, family, and practice plans. The parent trying to figure out why their child's flag keeps falling off mid-play. The quiet kid who hangs at the edge of the group, not quite sure if they belong. I wanted each of them to find something here, to feel seen, equipped, and encouraged.

This book isn't just about how to run a clean practice or win a few games. It's about what happens between those moments—the lessons kids carry long after the flags come off. They'll learn how to listen, lead, recover from mistakes, and celebrate each other's successes. You'll learn how to guide without shouting, teach without overwhelming, and build an environment where every player—no matter their skill—feels like part of the team.

And if you've ever worried that flag football is "too soft" or "not real football," let me assure you, spend five minutes trying to pull the flag of an eight-year-old running full speed, and you'll change your mind. It's strategic, fast-paced, and packed with just enough chaos to keep every adult on their toes. You'll laugh, sweat, and at some point, you'll find yourself shouting encouragements you didn't know you had in you. It's not about who can hit hardest; it's about who can work together best.

So what can you expect from the chapters ahead? Think of this book as your season-long teammate. We'll start with the basics: how the game works, what equipment you actually need (and what's a waste of money), and how to set the right tone from day one. Then we'll build step by step into practice plans, drills, plays, and game-day strategies that work for real teams with real kids. You'll also find sections on communication, leadership, sportsmanship, and even parent involvement because coaching kids means coaching families, too.

You won't need to memorize plays or master NFL-level strategy. You just need a willingness to learn and a sense of humor when things go sideways. Because they will. The ball will roll into the parking lot. Someone will forget their mouthguard. Half the team will show up late. And somehow, those chaotic, imperfect moments will become the memories everyone talks about for years. That's the magic of flag football; it teaches resilience wrapped in laughter.

So by the end of this book, my goal is simple: that you feel ready, not perfect. Ready to lead, ready to learn, ready to make the most of the short time you have with your team. You'll have tools, templates, and ideas, but more importantly, you'll have perspective; the understanding that every flag pulled, every high-five shared, and every lesson learned matters.

So take a breath. Lace up your sneakers. Grab the flags and the footballs. Whether you're a parent stepping onto the field for the first time, a volunteer looking to give back, or just someone curious about what makes this sport special, you're in the right place. Let's make this season unforgettable for the kids, for the families, and maybe, just a little bit, for ourselves too.

CHAPTER 1:
BUILDING A STRONG FOUNDATION

Perfection is not attainable, but if we chase perfection, we can catch excellence. – Vince Lombardi

The whistle blew, and twelve tiny bodies exploded across the field like popcorn kernels. Flags flapped, laughter echoed, and for a few wild seconds, nobody seemed entirely sure which direction the ball was supposed to go. I stood there, clipboard in hand, trying to look calm while silently wondering how professional coaches make this look easy. Then, right in the middle of that joyful chaos, something beautiful happened: a kid who'd been too shy to even say her name at the start of practice snagged her first flag. The look on her face said everything: confidence, surprise, and pure delight. That moment, more than any perfect play or shiny trophy, is what youth flag football is about.

This game isn't about hard hits or highlight reels. It's about seeing kids discover that they can do something they didn't think they could and parents high-fiving each other after a clean flag pull, about coaches realizing that teaching patience is harder and more rewarding than teaching routes. It's about laughter when a cone blows away mid-drill and the whole team chases it like it's the game-winning touchdown.

Flag football is football stripped to its heart. It's what happens when you take away the collisions and leave only the collaboration. When you remove the intimidation and make room for imagination. It's where strategy meets fun, and where every kid, fast or slow, quiet or loud, gets a real chance to shine. That's what hooked me from day one. And that's what this chapter is all about: understanding what youth flag football truly is, why it matters, and how to build the right foundation before you ever blow that first whistle.

Therefore, it's essential for us to look into the spirit of the game, the people who make it happen, and the reason this sport continues to grow on fields across the world. So grab your flags, loosen up that smile, and let's dive into what makes youth flag football one of the most unexpectedly powerful experiences you'll ever be part of.

ORIGINS OF FLAG FOOTBALL

Flag football started as an idea born out of necessity. During World War II, when resources were tight and full-contact sports were too risky for military bases, soldiers began improvising a safer version of football for recreation (Soule, n.d.). Instead of tackling, they used strips of cloth or rags tucked into their belts; if you pulled one, the play was dead. It was simple, smart, and safe. That creative twist laid the groundwork for what we now know as flag football.

When the war ended, the idea didn't fade. Colleges, local communities, and eventually youth leagues realized that this no-contact version of the game made football accessible to more people, especially kids and families who loved the spirit of the sport but not the injuries that came with it. By the 1960s and 70s, flag football leagues were springing up everywhere from schoolyards to recreation centers. The National Intramural and Recreational Sports Association (NIRSA) helped organize the first official college tournaments, while community centers began introducing children to the sport as a fun, inclusive way to stay active.

Fast forward to today, and flag football has grown into one of the fastest-expanding youth sports in the world. The NFL launched NFL FLAG in the 1990s, giving the sport a national platform and standardized rules. That single move turned weekend park games into organized leagues with thousands of teams, and now, with flag football even being recognized on the global stage, it's no longer a backyard pastime. It's a legitimate path for kids to learn teamwork, leadership, and skill development without the physical risks of tackle.

What began as an improvisation among soldiers has evolved into a movement rooted in inclusion. Flag football is now played in schools, community leagues, and even internationally, with the same goal that started it all: to make football fun, safe, and for everyone.

The heart of flag football has always been accessibility. The founders didn't set out to make a "lesser" version of football; they made a smarter one. They created a way to capture the strategy, excitement, and camaraderie of the sport without the fear of injury keeping kids or parents on the sidelines. In that sense, flag football isn't a downgrade; it's a doorway.

For many families, tackle football feels intimidating. The pads, the hits, the risk, it can all seem like too much, too soon. Flag football strips away the barriers and says, "Come as you are." You don't have to be the biggest, fastest, or toughest kid on the field. You just have to be willing to play, to learn, and to try. That's what makes it special.

As coaches, we see that firsthand. The kid who was too small to make the tackle team finds his stride as a receiver. The shy player learns to call plays and lead huddles. Parents who once sat on the sidelines, unsure of the rules, start volunteering, cheering, and learning right alongside their kids. Every flag pulled is a small victory; every laugh, a reminder of why we're out here.

FLAG FOOTBALL DEFINITION

So what exactly is youth flag football? To put it simply, it's a non-contact version of football designed for kids, where instead of tackling, players remove flags from the opponent's belt to stop a play. But underneath that simple rule lies something much deeper; it's a teaching ground for teamwork, communication, and confidence.

Modern youth flag football is intentionally structured to balance fun with fundamentals. The field is smaller, the plays are faster, and everyone touches the ball. It's a sport built around inclusion, not intimidation. Kids learn to pass, catch, defend, and most importantly, to work together. The focus isn't just on scoring points; it's on building character.

That's why we started here, with the "why" before the "how," because understanding the roots of flag football helps you appreciate its purpose. It wasn't designed to replace traditional football but simply to expand it, opening the doors wider so every child has a chance to experience what makes the game great.

Before we jump into the drills, diagrams, and play calls, take a moment to remember where this all began: a simple idea that football could be safe, creative, and fun for everyone. That same idea is what you, as a coach, parent, or player, now carry forward onto your field.

So, as we keep building, remember this: the story of flag football started with people adapting to their moment. And every time you gather your team, teach a new skill, or watch a kid's confidence grow, you're adding your own chapter to that same story.

The No-Contact Philosophy
Mention flag football to a die-hard football fan, and they might smirk until they watch it up close. A clean flag pull at full sprint, the perfect read on a pass, the sudden stop and pivot that leaves everyone gasping, those moments take precision, awareness, and control. The no-contact philosophy doesn't make the sport softer; it makes it sharper.

Removing tackling changed the game's focus. Defense became less about collision and more about positioning. Offense became less about overpowering and more about outsmarting. Players develop footwork, anticipation, and discipline in ways that translate far beyond the field. Every move demands focus, balance, and teamwork.

Safety might have started the shift, but confidence is what keeps it growing. Without the fear of hard hits, kids play freely. They experiment, take creative risks, and learn to adjust in real time. Mistakes become lessons instead of bruises, and success comes from mastering technique rather than brute force.

For coaches, this approach reshapes everything. Practices become about angles, timing, and communication. Instead of shouting through chaos, we slow the game down so kids can see how space opens up and how teamwork makes plays work. The lessons stick because players understand why something works, not just what to do. For instance, one moment still sticks with me. A player missed a flag, then instinctively reached out to steady the runner so he wouldn't fall. No whistle could've captured what that meant. That small act carried the spirit of flag football: competitive, respectful, connected. So the no-contact mindset builds more than athletes; it shapes character. Kids learn patience, awareness, and self-control, which are all skills that matter long after the final whistle. When someone questions whether flag football is real football, I just smile because while others chase impact, we're teaching impact of a different kind, the kind that lasts.

The Spirit of the Game
Every sport has rules, but flag football has something deeper: an unspoken rhythm that guides how the game is played and how players treat each other. It's the heartbeat of the sport, the part you can't measure on a scoreboard. The spirit of the game is what turns a bunch of kids running around in the grass into a team that laughs together, lifts each other up, and celebrates even the small wins.

One Saturday morning, I watched a team that hadn't won a single game all season finally score a touchdown. The scoreboard didn't matter; what mattered was the explosion of joy that followed. Players jumped, hugged, and high-fived like they had just won the championship. Parents cheered from the sidelines, some even tearing up. That moment summed up everything this sport stands for: effort, encouragement, and unity.

Flag football teaches lessons that stretch far beyond the field. Kids learn how to win with humility and lose with grace. They discover that good sportsmanship isn't just about shaking hands at the end of the game; it's about respect in every play, respect for teammates, opponents, referees, and themselves. The game demands cooperation over ego. You can't succeed alone, and that's the point.

Every practice and game becomes a classroom for character. A player might start the season focused only on catching touchdowns, but along the way, they learn how to block for a friend, how to give encouragement instead of criticism, and how to find joy in another teammate's success. That kind of growth builds not just better players but better people.

The beauty of flag football lies in its inclusivity. Every kid, no matter their size, gender, or experience level, has a role. A quiet player can become the team's most dependable flag puller; a kid who's never touched a football before can learn to throw a perfect spiral after a few practices. Everyone belongs, and everyone contributes.

As coaches and parents, we have a responsibility to protect that spirit. It's easy to get caught up in the competition, to chase wins or focus on stats, but the real victories are often invisible. They happen in the huddle when a player who made a mistake gets a pat on the back instead of a scolding. They happen when kids start to encourage each other without being told. That's the kind of culture that keeps them coming back season after season.

The spirit of the game also lives in how we handle challenges. There will be bad calls, missed flags, and frustrating plays. How teams respond defines them. The best moments I've seen didn't come from perfect games; they came from kids choosing to keep smiling, to try again, to cheer for one another even when they were behind. That resilience, that joy, is the true measure of success.

In flag football, teamwork isn't just a strategy, it's a language. Players learn to trust each other's instincts, to communicate with a glance or a hand signal, and to celebrate collective effort. They learn that every role matters. The quarterback can't shine without receivers running crisp routes, and defenders can't succeed without teammates holding their ground. When everyone plays their part, the team becomes something bigger than any single player.

That's the spirit we want to pass on. A spirit that values connection over competition, growth over glory, and participation over perfection. It's what turns a game into a community and a season into a memory that lasts a lifetime.

So as we move deeper into this journey, remember the heart of why we're here. Flag football gives us a space to teach values that matter, build confidence that lasts, and remind every player that their worth isn't defined by a scoreboard but by how they play the game.

WHO PLAYS AND WHY IT MATTERS

If you show up at a youth flag football field on a Saturday morning, you'll see a mix of people who perfectly capture what makes the sport so special. There are kids sprinting in mismatched socks, parents setting up folding chairs and socializing, coaches juggling clipboards and whistles, and siblings cheering (or occasionally stealing the ball between plays). It's a living picture of community, different people with different stories, all coming together around one simple goal: to play, to learn, and to grow.

Flag football attracts players of all kinds. Some are natural athletes looking for an outlet outside of tackle football. Others are kids who've never played a sport before but are curious and eager to belong. There are girls joining coed teams and discovering they can outrun anyone on the field. There are quiet kids who find their voice calling plays in the huddle, and energetic ones who learn patience through teamwork. Everyone has a place here.

Parents are just as much a part of the game. Some step in to coach; others learn the rules week by week from the sidelines. Many rediscover their own love for the sport through their children's experiences. What often starts as a way to keep kids active quickly becomes a family tradition. Friendships form, carpool groups turn into cheering sections, and game days become memories that shape childhood.

Coaches, many of them who happen to be volunteers, are the glue that holds it all together. They teach, motivate, organize, and sometimes even referee when needed. The best coaches don't just develop players; they develop people. They understand that a missed pass is less important than a lesson learned. Their patience, guidance, and encouragement become the foundation for every child's growth on and off the field.

And then there are the fans: grandparents with cameras, neighbors who stop by to watch, teachers who come to support their students. They're part of the ecosystem that gives the game its energy. When the sidelines erupt after a great play, it tells every kid on the field, "You matter."

This blend of players, parents, and mentors is what makes flag football bigger than a sport; it's a community in motion. The game creates a space where differences fade, and teamwork takes center stage. A field that starts as grass and chalk lines transforms into a meeting ground for lessons that last a lifetime: perseverance, respect, leadership, and joy.

That's why who plays matters just as much as how the game is played, because every person who shows up contributes to the culture. The laughter of the kids, the support of the parents, the dedication of the coaches—it all builds something worth protecting. When everyone invests, everyone wins. And that's the real victory flag football was built to create.

Key Takeaways
- **Teamwork drives success:** Flag football thrives on collaboration; every play depends on trust and communication.
- **Growth happens over time:** Skills develop one pass, one flag pull, and one lesson at a time.
- **Lead with heart:** Players remember how you encouraged them long after they forget the score.
- **Celebrate every step:** Recognize effort, discipline, and improvement as much as touchdowns.
- **Adapt and adjust:** Each practice brings surprises; weather, timing, or energy. Nevertheless, you need to learn to pivot with positivity.
- **Play with respect:** Good sportsmanship keeps the spirit of flag football alive and builds lasting character.

- **Keep learning:** Every game and every season is a chance to improve as a coach, player, or parent.

Take a breath and picture the field before the first whistle. Fresh grass, the buzz of excitement, and that small spark of uncertainty that comes before something great begins. This moment right here is where every season truly starts. Not with the first snap, but with the mindset you bring into it. Flag football is a journey built on growth, discovery, and connection. Progress doesn't arrive overnight; it comes through effort, laughter, and lessons that often show up in the middle of the chaos. You don't need to be an expert or have all the answers. What matters is being willing to learn, to show up, and to lead with patience and heart.

For coaches, that means teaching through encouragement and example. For parents, it's cheering with genuine joy, not pressure. For players, it's learning to trust yourself, your teammates, and the process. The victories that matter most won't always show up on the scoreboard; they'll live in the confidence, discipline, and character that form along the way.

The pages ahead will offer ideas, tools, and guidance to help you make the most of this sport. But the real power lies in the mindset you carry. Approach each practice as an opportunity to grow, not to prove. Treat every challenge as a chance to learn, not a reason to stop. When things don't go perfectly—and they won't—remember that progress hides in those rough edges. That's where resilience is built.

There will be messy days. Days when the drills go sideways, when the weather turns, when the kids forget half the gear. But those are the days that stretch your patience and deepen your purpose. Then there will also be those perfect moments, such as a smooth pass, a burst of laughter, a huddle that just feels right. Hold onto those. They're the reminders that this game is bigger than competition; it's about growth and shared experience.

Think of this journey as a sideline partner, *a quiet voice that reminds you of what really matters when the noise of the season gets loud. It's here to help you plan, teach, and lead with confidence, but more than that, it's here to keep your focus on the heart of it all: the people, the joy, and the lessons that will last far beyond the field.

So take that breath, tighten those laces, and step forward with purpose. You're not just preparing for a season, you're stepping into a journey that will shape memories, friendships, and character for years to come.

CHAPTER 2:
THE BIG BENEFITS

Sports do not build character. They reveal it.– Heywood Broun

The last chapter laid the foundation: understanding what flag football is, where it came from, and the spirit that keeps it alive. Now it's time to look at what the game actually does for the young people who play it because somewhere between all the drills, something powerful is happening. Kids are growing in confidence, in character, and in the quiet skills that will serve them long after the season ends.

If you've ever stood on the sidelines of a youth flag football game, you know what I mean. There's the kid who started the season afraid to catch the ball, now sprinting across the field with their head up and heart racing. There's the player who used to shy away from huddles, now calling out plays and helping teammates get into position. And there's always that parent who came to watch a game but leaves realizing they've witnessed their child become just a little braver, a little stronger, a little more alive.

This game does more than teach routes and flags; it teaches resilience, awareness, and the art of communication. Every dropped pass becomes a lesson in perseverance. Every clean flag pull becomes proof of focus and timing. Every high-five shared after a mistake reminds kids that effort matters more than perfection. Bit by bit, week by week, they build the kind of confidence that doesn't fade when the jerseys come off.

Flag football is where coordination meets courage, where teamwork shapes identity, and where fun builds the foundation for growth. It's a game that shows every child, no matter their size or background, that they belong. And through that belonging, something extraordinary happens: they start to believe in themselves.

In this chapter, we'll look closer at those benefits, the physical, social, and emotional skills this sport develops, and why parents, coaches, and communities are rallying behind it more than ever. After all, when we say flag football builds skills for life, we mean it.

PHYSICAL GROWTH AND COORDINATION

Flag football may not involve tackling, but it's still a full-body workout that challenges nearly every muscle group in a child's body. Each sprint, pivot, and quick flag pull strengthens their legs, core, and reflexes while improving agility and balance. Sports scientists often note that games built around short bursts of movement, like flag football, develop what's known as functional athleticism: coordination and control that translate to nearly every other sport or physical activity.

According to the American Council on Exercise, activities involving multidirectional running and reaction-based movement help improve both aerobic endurance and neuromuscular coordination. Flag football delivers both. The constant start-and-stop motion increases cardiovascular fitness, while the requirement to stay light on one's feet develops body awareness and timing. For young players, this type of physical conditioning lays the groundwork for lifelong health and agility.

A study published in the *Journal of Sports Science & Medicine* found that children who participate in structured team sports exhibit higher levels of motor skill competence and flexibility compared to those who don't. That's because flag football doesn't rely on repetitive drills alone; it naturally weaves movement into play. Running routes, pivoting to avoid defenders, or diving to pull a flag all challenge balance and reaction speed without kids even realizing they're training. It's learning through laughter and motion.

Beyond fitness, the sport helps develop essential movement patterns, such as acceleration, deceleration, and spatial awareness. Players learn how to move safely, plant their feet properly, and control their bodies under pressure. Coaches who emphasize good warm-ups and stretching routines further strengthen this foundation, reducing the risk of injuries and promoting long-term physical health.

Another underrated benefit is endurance. While the games are fast-paced, they demand repeated bursts of energy over time. That blend of aerobic and anaerobic exercise builds stamina. Kids who start the season winded by halftime often end it running full speed through every play. That physical growth isn't just measurable, it's visible, week after week, in the way they move with more confidence and coordination.

Furthermore, since flag football is a non-contact sport, it gives young athletes a safe space to explore physicality without fear. They can focus on refining their movements instead of bracing for hits. This environment lets them take healthy risks by trying new techniques, changing direction sharply, and reaching higher for passes while their bodies learn control and precision. It's physical education disguised as fun.

In essence, flag football trains the body and the brain simultaneously. Every run, every flag pull, and every quick decision builds muscle memory, focus, and control. It's a sport that molds athletic ability through motion, not monotony, giving every child the chance to grow stronger, faster, and more confident in their own skin.

Social and Emotional Development

Flag football may start as a simple game, but beneath the bright jerseys and fluttering flags, it's a social classroom. Every activity becomes an opportunity to teach communication, teamwork, and emotional intelligence. It's one of the few sports where kids have to rely completely on awareness of others reading faces, listening for cues, and adjusting their actions to support the team.

You can spot the lessons happening in real time. A child drops a pass and immediately hears a teammate say, "Shake it off, you've got the next one." That single sentence does more for confidence than any pep talk ever could. Another child, usually the loudest voice on the field, learns the importance of letting others lead a play. These little exchanges are the building blocks of empathy and leadership.

Flag football demands communication. Since there's no heavy gear or constant physical clashes, players learn to talk, to strategize, signal, and motivate each other. They learn the art of listening, too. The best teams aren't just the fastest; they're the ones that listen to one another. When kids begin to understand that good communication wins games, they carry that same lesson into classrooms, friendships, and even at home.

The sport also teaches emotional balance. Losing a game, missing a flag, or getting outrun by an opponent can sting, but flag football creates a space where disappointment becomes a catalyst for growth instead of defeat. Coaches who model calm and positivity after setbacks teach players how to handle life's tougher moments with grace. Over time, kids learn to manage frustration, celebrate others' success, and bounce back stronger.

One of the most rewarding aspects of coaching is watching relationships form on the field. Kids who barely knew each other at the start of the season begin to share inside jokes, small victories, and mutual trust. Shy players open up, talk more, and begin to take ownership of the game. For some children, that sense of belonging can be life-changing. It's no exaggeration to say that a single season of flag football can build friendships that outlast the sport itself.

Parents notice it, too. The quiet car rides home become lively recaps of teamwork, not just scores. Kids talk about helping a teammate or making a good play as a group. That shift from "I" to "we" is the clearest proof that something deeper is taking root.

At its core, flag football gives kids a safe, joyful arena to learn what it means to connect, cooperate, and care. Those lessons don't fade when the season ends; they echo in how they treat others, solve problems, and build relationships for the rest of their lives.

Inclusivity and Opportunity for All

One of the greatest strengths of flag football is how it opens the field to everyone. You don't have to be tall, strong, or the fastest kid out there to make a difference. Every player has a role, and every role matters. This sport levels the playing field literally and figuratively, creating a space where every child can contribute, feel valued, and succeed in their own way.

In traditional contact sports, physical size or strength often determines who stands out. In flag football, success depends more on creativity, teamwork, and awareness. A smaller player with quick feet and good instincts can be just as impactful as someone faster or stronger. It's a sport that rewards effort and strategy just as much as raw athleticism.

Inclusivity isn't just about ability, it's about access. Flag football has become one of the most inclusive youth sports because of how easy it is to join. All you need is a ball, a few flags, and some open space. There's no expensive equipment or complicated gear list, which makes it accessible to families from all backgrounds. Many communities have started coed leagues, bringing boys and girls together on the same teams, where they learn respect and teamwork across differences.

Some of the most inspiring players you'll meet aren't the ones scoring touchdowns but the ones discovering their confidence for the first time. I've seen shy kids blossom into leaders after realizing they can read plays and direct teammates. I've seen kids who struggled in school find pride and focus in the field. One coach told me about a player who began the season too nervous to touch the ball but ended it leading a game-winning drive. Those moments are reminders that inclusivity isn't just a goal, it's the foundation of what this sport is built on.

For parents, the inclusive nature of flag football is a gift. It teaches their children that effort matters more than ability, and that being part of something bigger than themselves can be deeply rewarding. For coaches, it's an opportunity to nurture every player, not just the standouts, and show that leadership comes in many forms. The quiet, observant kid might become your best strategist. The energetic chatterbox might turn into the heartbeat of the team.

Flag football builds belonging. When kids see that everyone, regardless of size, gender, or experience, gets a chance to play and make an impact, it changes how they view competition. Winning feels different when it's shared, and success feels deeper when everyone contributes. That sense of unity is what keeps players coming back year after year.

In a world where comparison often overshadows cooperation, flag football stands out as a reminder that teamwork, respect, and inclusion can create something truly powerful. The sport's real victory isn't in the score, it's in the smiles, the shared effort, and the confidence that every player carries long after the final whistle.

So, from physical development to emotional growth, and now inclusivity, each layer of flag football reveals how deeply connected the game is to real life. The sport doesn't just train the body or the mind, it molds the whole person. Kids learn movement, discipline, teamwork, and belonging all at once. Each section of this journey so far has built toward something greater: the kind of character that carries through both victory and defeat.

This next part of the story dives into that exact spirit. Everything else points to one truth: flag football thrives when the joy of the game takes center stage. Before we translate to the finer details of scores and competition, it's worth remembering why this game captures hearts in the first place. It's the fun, the character, and the love for the play that truly make it special.

Character and Fun Over Competition

If there's one thing that separates flag football from most youth sports, it's the way it reminds kids, parents, and coaches alike that the game is supposed to be fun. Sure, every player wants to win, and competition has its place, but in flag football, character always comes first. The laughs between teammates, the cheers from the sidelines, and the small gestures of sportsmanship often matter far more than the final score.

You can see it in those little moments, such as the high-fives after a good play, the helping hand extended when someone trips, the grins exchanged between players from opposing teams. These are not just glimpses of good manners; they're snapshots of character in motion. Kids begin to understand that respect, honesty, and teamwork are habits that they can practice and develop one play at a time.

There's a story from a local league that still sticks with me. Two teams were tied with seconds left on the clock. The quarterback launched a perfect pass to a player sprinting toward the end zone. Just as the flag was about to be pulled, the runner stumbled and fell short. Instead of celebrating the near win, both teams rushed over to help him up. The game ended in laughter instead of frustration, and everyone walked away smiling. That's flag football at its best—where joy wins out over ego.

For coaches, moments like that are reminders that they're not just shaping athletes, they're shaping people. Teaching kids how to compete with integrity, handle disappointment, and celebrate others' success is as valuable as any drill or playbook. Parents, too, play a vital role. When they model calmness on the sidelines and cheer for effort rather than outcome, they reinforce what the sport is truly about.

And let's not forget the simple, contagious fun of the game itself. The energy of a pickup match at the park, the sound of sneakers on grass, the laughter that comes after a fumbled handoff, all of it builds memories that outlast statistics. Kids who enjoy the process of playing grow into adults who value teamwork, discipline, and balance. They carry that lighthearted spirit into everything they do.

Flag football teaches that winning is great, but growing is greater. The victories that matter most can't always be measured on a scoreboard, they're seen in confidence, kindness, and character that take root over time. When kids learn to play hard, laugh freely, and lift others along the way, they've already won something far more important than a trophy.

Long-Term Benefits

So, as we have briefly established, what happens on the field doesn't stay there. The lessons kids learn through flag football follow them into every part of their lives: classrooms, friendships, families, and even future careers. The discipline it takes to show up for practice, the courage to try again after missing a catch, and the patience to work as a team all build habits that last far beyond childhood.

Physically, players develop fitness habits that carry into adulthood. Once a child discovers how good it feels to move, to sprint freely, or to set and chase a goal, exercise becomes less of a chore and more of a lifestyle. The coordination, strength, and endurance built through flag football often give kids a foundation that helps them thrive in other sports and activities.

Mentally, the game instills resilience. Every player faces setbacks: missed flags, dropped passes, or close losses, and learns to process those moments without giving up. They start to see failure not as something to fear but as part of the journey. This mindset becomes powerful in academics and everyday challenges, where perseverance matters more than perfection.

Socially, flag football nurtures leadership and communication skills. Kids who learn to encourage teammates and strategize together are unknowingly training for future teamwork in school projects, jobs, and relationships. They begin to understand the value of collaboration and accountability, and that real leadership often looks like service, empathy, and consistency.

And emotionally, the sport gives kids a place to belong. In an age where many children struggle with confidence or connection, flag football offers a safe space to grow through encouragement, laughter, and shared goals. That sense of belonging can build lifelong confidence and self-worth.

Flag football doesn't just create better players, it shapes better people. The habits of focus, cooperation, and joy they learn on the field echo into adulthood. Decades later, they may forget the scores, but they'll never forget the lessons, the teamwork, or the thrill of running free under an open sky.

Key Takeaways
- **Flag football builds habits for life.** The discipline, teamwork, and resilience learned on the field translate into school, friendships, and future careers.
- **Health and fitness take root early.** Regular movement, coordination, and exercise through flag football help build lifelong physical well-being.
- **Failure becomes growth.** Kids learn to recover from mistakes, keep trying, and focus on progress rather than perfection.
- **Leadership emerges naturally.** Every player gets the chance to communicate, guide, and uplift others; skills that carry far beyond the game.
- **Belonging creates confidence.** A supportive, inclusive environment helps children feel valued, building character and lasting self-esteem.

As the whistle blows and the field clears, what remains is far more than a game. It's the laughter that still echoes, the friendships that linger, and the quiet lessons that settle in long after the flags are packed away. Every moment adds to something bigger, which is the kind of growth that lasts a lifetime.

This journey has shown that flag football is more than competition; it's a connection, community, and character in motion. When kids leave the field smiling, standing taller, and ready to face new challenges, that's the real scoreboard. So, as we move forward, we'll explore how these lessons expand beyond the sidelines, shaping not only players but also the culture and the future of youth sports.

CHAPTER 3
NAVIGATING LEAGUE TYPES, GEAR, AND FIRST-DAY ESSENTIALS

The will to win is important, but the will to prepare is vital.
— Joe Paterno

By now, we've seen how flag football builds confidence, character, and connection. The spirit is there, for instance, the drive, the joy, and the teamwork, but every great game also needs structure. That's where preparation comes in. The difference between a chaotic first season and a rewarding one often comes down to understanding the basics: which league format you're in, what gear you actually need, and how to bring a brand-new team together on day one.

So now this is where excitement meets logistics. It's the practical side of passion, the part that turns enthusiasm into smooth execution, because let's face it, as any coach or parent knows, the first day of flag football season can feel like organized chaos. Flags everywhere, kids asking which cone is which, parents searching for missing mouth guards, it's a rite of passage for every beginner. However, with a bit of guidance, that chaos becomes confidence.

So now, we'll break down what every coach, parent, and player should know before stepping onto the field. We'll explore the different league formats: 5-on-5, 6-on-6, and 7-on-7, so you can walk in knowing exactly how your game will flow. We'll unpack the essential gear checklist so nobody's scrambling to borrow a flag belt at kickoff. Then we'll walk through that all-important first day, the moment when nervous kids turn into teammates.

Think of this as your preseason playbook; all you need is enough information to get you prepared, because when everyone shows up ready physically, mentally, and logistically, the real magic of the game can shine through. Whether you're coaching your first team, signing your child up for their debut season, or just curious about how it all works, this is where you get your footing.

Flag football thrives on readiness, rhythm, and relationships. So let's get you set up, geared up, and ready to lead your team with confidence. The whistle's about to blow, so it's time to step onto the field and make it count.

League Formats

Youth flag football uses a few common formats, each with its own flow, space requirements, and coaching implications. Knowing the core differences helps you plan practices, build plays that work, and avoid scrambling in the first game. Below is a practical, coach-friendly guide to the three most common formats and how to adapt to each one.

Comparison Snapshot: League Formats

Format	Typical Ages	Field Dimensions	Team Size	Playstyle	Coaching Focus
5-on-5	5-8 years	40–50 yards long, narrower field	8-12 total players	Fast-paced, high-touch, simplified plays	Fundamentals, frequent rotation, hands-on learning
6-on-6	8–10 years	50-60 yards long	9–14 total players	Balanced Mix of Speed and Structure	Spacing, short passing routes, early play-calling skills
7-on-7	10–14 years	60–80 yards long	10-16 total players	Spread formations, complex reads, more strategy	Timing, communication, advanced situational drills

Coach's Tip: Each format builds on the previous one. Think of 5-on-5 as learning the alphabet, 6-on-6 as forming sentences, and 7-on-7 as writing the story. The structure grows, but the heart of the game never changes.

ESSENTIAL EQUIPMENT CHECKLIST FOR KIDS AND COACHES

Preparation starts long before the first whistle. The best seasons often begin with something as simple as being organized. Having the right equipment doesn't just make practices run smoother, it keeps kids safe, engaged, and confident. This section breaks down what every player, coach, and parent should have ready before game day, why it matters, and a few tips that save both time and money.

Player Essentials

Item	Purpose	Notes & Tips
Flag, Belt, & Flags	The heart of the game, used instead of tackling.	Make sure the flags are secure but easy to pull. Avoid belts that twist or slide. Keep a few extras on hand.
Football	Used for passing, handoffs, and drills.	Size varies by age: Pee Wee for ages 5–8, Junior for 9–12, Youth for 13–14. Label the ball to avoid mix-ups.
Jerseys & Pinnies	Distinguishes teams during games.	Choose lightweight, breathable fabric. Avoid dark colors in hot weather.
Mouthguard	Protects teeth and mouth.	Mandatory in most leagues. Molded mouthguards fit better and stay secure.
Athletic Shorts or Pants (No Pockets)	Prevents fingers from catching on fabric during flag pulls.	Some leagues ban pockets altogether. Tape or turn inside-out if needed.

Cleats or Turf Shoes	Improves traction and movement.	Rubber cleats only; metal is not allowed. Check laces and fit regularly.
Water Bottle	Keeps players hydrated throughout practice and games.	Label clearly. Encourage kids to drink small sips often, not chug at once.

Coach and Team Essentials

Item	Purpose	Notes & Tips
Whistle	Keeps drills and games organized.	Use short blasts for attention and long for transitions. Always carry a backup.
Cones or Field Markers	Define boundaries, routes, and drills.	Bright colors work best. Carry a mesh bag for easy cleanup.
Clipboards or Playbooks	Keep plays and rosters handy.	Use waterproof sleeves or laminated sheets for rainy days.
Mesh Bags or Bins	For storing flags, balls, and cones.	Label gear to stay organized. Create a team checklist for load-out after every game.
First Aid Kit	For minor scrapes, sprains, or blisters.	Include bandages, cold packs, and antiseptic wipes. Know where it's stored at all times.
Extra Gear	Backups for anything that breaks or goes missing.	A few spare flags, belts, and mouthguards go a long way in saving time.
Team Roaster & Contact Sheet	Keeps Communication Easy	Have both digital and paper versions for quick reference.

Budget-Friendly Tips

- **Buy in bulk** through league partners or local sports stores; many offer team discounts.
- **Share gear**: Encourage families to contribute extras like cones or flags.
- **DIY solutions**: Old t-shirts can become practice jerseys; PVC pipes can mark sidelines.
- **Used gear programs**: Many leagues and community centers run exchange bins for gently used items.
- **Label everything**: It's cheaper to label now than replace later. Use permanent markers or color-coded tape.

Coach's Corner: Organization on Game Day

- Pack the night before. Use a checklist so nothing gets left behind.
- Assign one player each week as the "gear captain" to help track equipment.
- Keep one labeled bin for game gear and another for practice gear.
- Arrive 20–30 minutes early to set up cones and test the field layout.
- Store all important items (keys, first aid, roster) in one waterproof pouch.

Essentially, consistency beats chaos. When everyone knows where the gear is, how it's packed, and who's responsible for what, you create more time for the fun part, which is playing the game.

INTRODUCING THE TEAM - FIRST-DAY ICEBREAKERS AND BUILDING TRUST

The gear's packed, the cones are lined up, and the air hums with that first-day energy, the kind where excitement and nerves blur together. You can feel it before anyone even steps on the field. The parents are hovering with cameras and water bottles, the kids are glancing around trying to read the room, and you, as the coach, are standing there knowing that whatever happens today will set the tone for everything that follows.

That first whistle isn't just the start of practice. It's the start of trust. Furthermore, the first day is less about drills and more about belonging. Kids might not remember what play you ran, but they'll remember how they felt being part of something new. That's your job to create an atmosphere where they can breathe, laugh, and open up. If you can make them comfortable now, the rest of the season will take care of itself.

Start with a smile and something light. For instance, you can joke about how shiny the new flags look or how someone's cleats are probably faster than the coach's. Humor breaks tension faster than any warm-up lap. Call players by name if you know them; if not, learn them quickly. Kids feel seen when you say their names; it's a small detail that builds trust instantly.

Once everyone's relaxed, gather the team for a quick talk. Keep it short and real: "We're going to learn, we're going to mess up, and we're going to have fun doing it." Tell them mistakes and losing aren't the problem, but quitting is. Tell them every voice matters. In flag football, no one rides the bench forever, and that's what makes it special.

Then, get them moving. Standing around too long lets nerves creep back in, so start with games that blend motion and laughter.

The Name Game Toss works wonders. Form a circle, toss a football, and say your name before you throw. On the next round, call out the person's name you're passing to. Before long, they're remembering names and laughing at the inevitable fumbles.

Cone Dash Relay is another gem. Set up a zigzag of cones, divide the team into small groups, and turn it into a race. Have them grab a flag at the last cone before sprinting back. It's a burst of energy that breaks the ice, builds teamwork, and gives you a peek at each player's comfort level.

For something calmer, try Teammate Match-Up. Ask players to find someone who shares a favorite food, superhero, or hobby. It sounds simple, but it sparks genuine conversation, and that's what you want on day one.

Wrap up the fun with something creative like a Team Cheer Challenge. Give them a few minutes to come up with a chant, handshake, or even a goofy dance. Perform it at the end of practice. It might sound silly, but you'll see confidence bloom right there in the laughter.

Now that the energy's up and everyone's smiling, start planting the seeds of team culture. Praise effort out loud. When a player helps another up, point it out. When someone listens well or cheers for a teammate, make sure everyone hears your appreciation. Kids pick up faster on what you celebrate than on what you correct.

And remember that your calm is contagious. When things go wrong (and they will), your reaction becomes the lesson.

Stay patient, stay playful, and keep the atmosphere light. A good coach knows that growth happens somewhere between structure and freedom.

Also, every team has that one quiet kid who hangs back a little, watching more than joining in. Don't rush them, just make sure they're never invisible. Pair them with friendly teammates, give them small wins early, and check in privately afterward. Sometimes all it takes is, "You looked more confident today. Keep that up." Those small, personal moments are what bring shy kids out of their shells.

By the end of that first day, don't aim for perfection. Aim for connection. If your players walk off the field smiling, high-fiving, or talking about when they'll see each other again, you've already won. Skills will come with time; belonging starts right here.

Coach's Corner: End the first practice with a simple circle huddle. Ask each player to name one thing they enjoyed, one thing they learned, or one teammate who made them laugh. It's quick, but it plants something powerful called gratitude, attention, and unity. That's the foundation of every great season.

COMMON MYTHS AND MISCONCEPTIONS

When a sport grows rapidly, so do stories and assumptions. Flag football is no exception. New coaches, parents, and even seasoned volunteers often bring baggage to the field; ideas that sound convincing but don't hold up once the whistle blows. We need to clear those up so we can prepare you. Understanding the real risks, the real wins, and the real limits helps you lead with clarity and compassion.

1. You Need Football Experience to Coach

Many people assume coaching requires years of playing experience or some secret playbook knowledge. That scares away the best volunteers: parents who care most but think they're not qualified. In reality, coaching young kids demands patience, structure, and a willingness to learn more than it demands a background in college football. The most effective youth coaches are those who can organize practices, keep things fun, and teach basic skills step by step. Experience helps, but heart and consistency matter more. A few truths to hold:

- You can coach by learning with the kids. Treat practices as experiments, try a drill, see how it lands, tweak it.
- Use simple scripts for common moments. A short warm-up script, a drill rotation plan, and a clear substitution method beat complexity every time.
- Recruit helpers. Great coaches surround themselves with people who can manage water, hand out flags, and calm parents. It multiplies your impact.

2. Winning Is the Only Thing That Matters

From competitive parents to self-imposed pressure, the idea that the scoreboard defines success circulates widely. However, for youth flag football, success lies in development, effort, team culture, and fun. Wins are great, but they are an accident if they come at the cost of the team's character or the players' long-term love of the game. A few truths to note:

- Define success beyond scores: Track improvement in effort, attendance, and confidence.

- Celebrate small wins: Consistency, good communication, and sportsmanship.
- Communicate values with parents early. If everyone shares the same vision, it prevents sideline pressure and keeps the focus on growth.

3. Flag Football Is Watered-Down Tackle Football

Some critics treat flag as a lesser version of tackle football, as if removing contact removes the essence of the sport. This couldn't be further from the truth; flag football changes what the sport emphasizes. It brings strategy, skill, and awareness to the front. Players learn agility, timing, and communication in ways that tackle can obscure. Different does not mean lesser.

- Flag trains different muscles and instincts. For instance, footwork, route running, and pass timing become crucial.
- Many skills learned in flag translate directly to tackle play later on, but flag also opens the game to kids who would never try tackle.
- Respect the unique challenges of the flag. Timing and spacing are skills that take practice and coaching, just like any other technique.

4. You Need Expensive Gear to Participate

Parents often assume they must buy the latest equipment or brand-name cleats to be ready for season one. Fortunately, flag football thrives on accessibility. Basic, safe gear covers most needs. Many leagues supply team pinnies and sometimes flags. Smart buying beats expensive buying. Take note:

- Start with the essentials: a properly sized football, a secure flag belt, a mouth guard, and comfortable shoes.
- Borrow, swap, and recycle. Local programs often use gear programs or community bins.
- Quality matters, but brand does not. A well-fitting mouth guard and correctly sized ball matter more than a logo.

5. Rules Will Be the Same Across Leagues

Assuming all leagues play by the same rulebook leads to confusion and frustration. It's a common source of sideline arguments and coach stress. In all honesty, rules vary. Field sizes, substitution methods, blitz allowances, and even flag rules differ from one league to another. The smart coach finds out early and trains accordingly. A few facts to consider:

- Confirm your league rules in writing before practice one.
- Practice the odd rules repeatedly so kids know what to expect.
- Keep a one-page cheat sheet for the most common differences to avoid last-minute scrambling.

When flag football began as an improvised answer to risk and resource shortages, pioneers tried things that later proved flawed. They used rags tied to belts that came loose, fields too small for proper play that encouraged collisions, and inconsistent scoring rules that confused players and parents. Those early failures mattered. They forced leagues to standardize belts and flags, define field sizes that promote spacing, and agree on clear rule sets. The modern game grew from trial and error. That history teaches coaches a valuable mindset: expect to iterate

and improve. These historical events gave us a few important things to learn:
1. Standardize equipment early. Loose flags and mismatched belts break rhythm.
2. Size matters. Too-small fields compress play and increase accidental contact.
3. Clear rules prevent arguments and build trust. When everyone knows the baseline, referees can manage the game fairly.

Furthermore, coaching is a craft shaped by mistakes. You will forget mouth guards, misjudge a drill, choose a play that flops, and face days when the kids are checked out. That is not failure; it is data. Every misstep tells you something about your players, your plan, or your communication.

So this is how you turn errors into progress:
1. Debrief quickly and kindly. After a rough practice, say what went well and what you'll change next time.
2. Keep notes. A small notebook tracking which drills landed and which sank saves time and stress.
3. Share responsibility. Ask assistant coaches or energetic parents for honest feedback and help with adjustments.
4. Normalize mistakes. Teach players that the best players recover, learn, and try again.

Practical Expectations for the Season's Rhythm

Here are some realistic rhythms and what to expect week to week:

- Week 1 to 3: Setup and discovery. Players get used to gear, spacing, and basic plays. Expect uneven attendance and jittery energy. Focus on fun and safety.
- Week 4 to 6: Momentum builds. Skills start to stick, and team chemistry grows. Add simple game concepts and structured scrimmages.
- Week 7 to 10: Sharpening. Focus on situational drills, rotations, and consistency. Start introducing a small playbook if appropriate.
- Postseason or wrap-up: Reflect and celebrate. Recognize gains, hand out simple awards or certificates, and gather parent feedback for next season.

In a nutshell, flag football is forgiving. It rewards patience, curiosity, and creativity. If you walk into a season with clear expectations and a calm approach to mistakes, you will find growth in places you did not expect. Encourage effort, coach with humility, and remember to celebrate. When parents, coaches, and players share that mindset, the season becomes less about perfect plays and more about meaningful progress.

Coach's Note: The field is where we learn faster than anywhere else. Treat mistakes like practice for life.

Your First-Season Game Plan

So now, the first day might end with smiles and laughter, but what happens next determines whether that spark becomes a steady flame. The real magic of flag football doesn't come from one good practice; it comes from rhythm. From showing up, week after week, and watching those shy faces turn into confident grins. That's where coaching becomes something deeper than drills and cones.

So now you've introduced the team, built some trust, and seen a few personalities emerge. Maybe you've already spotted your natural leaders; the kids who encourage others without being asked. Maybe you've noticed who needs a little more time to warm up. Either way, this is where you start turning that collection of individuals into a team.

The early weeks of a season are all about balance. You're setting routines, building habits, and creating structure, but still keeping things light enough for fun. Think of it as laying the groundwork for something that can grow naturally. The trick isn't to overwhelm your players with too much information too soon. Instead, it's about finding a rhythm that keeps everyone learning without burning out.

Start each session with something familiar. Kids love predictability. It gives them confidence. Whether it's a group warm-up song, a short team chant, or a fun drill they already know, small rituals create unity. They say, *we're a team now.*

Then, gradually layer in the new material, such as skills, plays, and small strategies. Build from the simple to the complex. A good coach doesn't rush the foundation. Every clean route, every sharp flag pull, every small success deserves attention. When players feel their progress is noticed, they try harder without being told.

And don't forget the parents, they're part of the team too. A quick update after practice or a cheerful group message about what the kids learned goes a long way. It keeps families invested and creates a community around your squad. When parents echo your values at home, the lessons stick.

You'll also start noticing how practice energy shifts as weeks go on. The early-season jitters fade into familiarity. Laughter becomes teamwork. Those moments when kids call out each other's names, celebrate flags, or huddle up on their own, those are your silent wins. They mean your culture is taking root.

However, here's the secret that separates great coaches from good ones: consistency. The best teams aren't built from big speeches; they're built from small, repeated actions that build trust. Show up the same way every time: steady, patient, and positive. When players know what to expect from you, they feel safe enough to give their best.

Keep an open ear, too. Sometimes the best adjustments come from listening, whether it's a kid suggesting a new warm-up or a parent mentioning their child felt nervous. Little insights like that make a big difference. It's all part of the learning curve, not just for the team, but for you as the coach.

By midseason, you'll notice something special. The kids who once hid behind others are now calling for the ball. The team that stumbled through the first relay now moves like one unit. That transformation doesn't happen by accident; it happens because you built an environment where growth feels natural.

So as you move through your first season, remember this: You're not just teaching football but teaching how to work together, how to fail well, how to keep showing up. Every flag pulled, every laugh shared, every lesson learned, these moments are shaping something far bigger than a game.

Also, remember to stay steady, kind, and always celebrate the small wins. Great teams aren't built in a day; they're built in moments that seem small at first but end up lasting a lifetime.

Key Takeaways
- **Rhythm builds champions.** The heart of a great season lies in the steady rhythm of consistency. Each week adds another brick to the foundation of teamwork, confidence, and trust.
- **Connection before correction.** Kids learn best when they feel safe and supported. When you take time to know their names, laugh with them, and celebrate their effort, correction becomes growth, not criticism.
- **Small moments shape big outcomes.** A compliment after a clean flag pull, a quiet word to a nervous player, a team chant after practice, these are the seeds that grow into lifelong confidence.
- **Parents are teammates too.** When you include families in the journey, your message travels beyond the field. A quick text or post-practice chat turns parents into allies, echoing the same lessons of effort, respect, and joy.
- **Consistency beats intensity.** A calm, predictable presence inspires more trust than any fiery pep talk ever

could. Your steadiness tells your team that even on tough days, they're safe to keep trying.
- **The goal isn't perfection, it's belonging.** Every laugh, every mistake, every shared victory moves your team closer together. A season built on belonging always succeeds, no matter the scoreboard.

Reflect on this: every season starts with uncertainty, but ends with growth for both players and coaches. If your team walks away loving the game, supporting each other, and believing in themselves, then you've already won regardless of the result on the pitch.

CHAPTER 4
MASTERING RULES - CLARITY AND CONFIDENCE FOR KIDS AND ADULTS

It's not the size of the player in the game, but the size of the game in the player. – Unknown

Every coach, parent, and player has lived through that moment when the whistle blows, everyone freezes, and no one seems to know what just happened. A touchdown is called back. A flag is missing. Someone yells, "That's not fair!" while the referee explains a rule that sounds like it was written in another language. Those moments are part of the early growing pains of any sport, and flag football is not an exception; they usually have nothing to do with athletic ability. They come from one simple thing: not knowing the rules well enough.

Understanding the rules of youth flag football isn't about memorizing a manual. It's about creating clarity. It's about giving kids and adults a shared language so the game flows smoothly. When the rules are clear, kids play with confidence. They stop second-guessing themselves. Parents cheer with understanding instead of confusion. Coaches lead with calm authority rather than hesitation. The whole experience becomes better, cleaner, safer, and more enjoyable.

The truth is, most parents and even new coaches don't start out as rule experts. Many are former players who remember fragments of tackle football rules or people who've never played at all but love being involved. Youth flag football varies widely across leagues: **NFL FLAG, YMCA, i9 Sports, Upward,** and local recreational divisions all tweak their regulations slightly. That means what's legal in one game might draw a penalty in another. Without proper orientation, even well-meaning coaches end up frustrated when plays get called back for something they didn't know existed.

That's why it's essential for us to create this section to take all that confusion and turn it into clarity. So for now, we'll break the game down piece by piece, from how a play begins to how a touchdown is scored. You'll learn what the referee is looking for, what players should watch out for, and how to spot small mistakes before they become penalties. We'll walk through examples you'll actually see on the field, so when something strange happens mid-game, you'll know exactly what to do and how to explain it calmly.

Think of this as your on-field translator, a guide that turns the formal rulebook into plain English. You don't need to be an expert; you just need to know enough to keep the game flowing and your players focused. Because when adults understand the rules, the kids get to focus on what matters most, which is playing, learning, and having fun.

Before diving into specifics, it helps to understand why rule clarity is so vital in youth sports. Children thrive on structure. It gives them a sense of fairness and predictability. When they understand why something is a penalty or how a play resets, they build discipline and respect for the process. It also prevents frustration from turning into blame, the silent killer of teamwork. Coaches who take time to explain the "why" behind calls often notice better sportsmanship and fewer emotional outbursts from their players.

We'll also unpack some of the most misunderstood calls, such as flag guarding, illegal contact, forward passes, and substitution rules, and then we explain them with real-game situations. For example, what happens when a flag falls off mid-play? What if two players accidentally bump while reaching for the same flag? What if a pass hits the ground but the flag is pulled right after? By using realistic examples and league comparisons, you'll start to see patterns in how referees think and how the game maintains fairness.

As you move through this chapter, remember this: rule mastery isn't about control, it's about freedom. The more you understand how the game works, the less you have to think about it. The rules stop being obstacles and start becoming the rhythm that carries every play forward. When that happens, confidence takes over, and that's when youth flag football becomes what it was always meant to be: organized chaos with purpose.

The Roots of the Game: From Tackle to Flag

Before we dive into the modern rules of youth flag football, it helps to look back at the game it was born from. Traditional football began in the late 1800s, when it evolved out of rugby. Back then, there were no helmets, no padding, and almost no safety standards. The early rules favored physical collisions and raw strength over strategy. Players could grab, shove, or even wrestle opponents to the ground to gain possession of the ball. The result was a game that was thrilling but dangerous. Records from that era show hundreds of injuries and even deaths among college players, which eventually pushed universities and governing bodies to step in and reform the sport.

One of the key reformers was Walter Camp, often called the father of American football. Camp helped bring order to chaos by introducing rules that shaped the modern game. He created the line of scrimmage, standardized the number of downs, and introduced systems for scoring and possession. These innovations brought structure and fairness, but football still remained a full-contact sport. As it grew in popularity, especially in schools and colleges, the need for safer versions became clear.

That is where flag football found its place. It was created to preserve the strategy and excitement of football while removing the tackling and heavy physical contact. Instead of bringing an opponent to the ground, players would remove a flag attached to a belt to signify a tackle. This simple change transformed everything. Suddenly, kids, families, and even adults who were hesitant about tackle football could enjoy the same teamwork and competition without the high risk of injury.

The first official flag football games appeared around the 1940s, largely played by military personnel who wanted a recreational, low-risk version of football during downtime. After the war, the idea spread to schools, community programs, and youth organizations. Over the decades, leagues formalized, rules were standardized, and governing bodies like the NFL FLAG program helped bring unity and safety to the sport. What started as a creative adjustment became one of the most inclusive and fastest-growing youth sports in America (Dawg, 2024).

Understanding this evolution helps explain why certain flag football rules exist today. Every restriction, from the no-contact policy to flag-guarding penalties, has its roots in player protection and fairness. The absence of tackling shifts focus from brute force to agility, awareness, and teamwork. Where tackle football rewards physical dominance, flag football celebrates precision, timing, and communication. The result is a version of the sport that keeps the spirit of competition alive while allowing every child, regardless of size or experience, to participate safely.

So before you step onto the field, remember this: flag football wasn't created to water down the game; it was created to open it up. It's football reimagined for learning, growth, and inclusion. Once you understand the roots, the rules you're about to learn make perfect sense.

YOUTH FLAG FOOTBALL RULES

When you first look at a flag football field, it can feel like organized chaos. Cones mark invisible lines, players scatter into positions, and a referee with a whistle seems to speak a different language. But once you understand the logic behind how a play begins, unfolds, and ends, that chaos starts to form a rhythm. Every whistle, every flag pull, and every reset has a purpose. Let's explore that and simplify what feels complex, so anyone can follow with confidence.

How a Play Begins

Every flag football play starts with a **snap**, which is when the center passes the ball between their legs to the quarterback to begin the action. The snap can't happen until both teams are set and still for at least one second. This rule teaches patience, discipline, and teamwork. It also ensures that both teams have an equal opportunity to react when the play begins. If a player moves early, it's called a **false start**, and the team loses yardage or replays the down, depending on the league rules.

The moment the ball is snapped, the play is live. Offensive players move to execute their routes or handoffs, while defenders react to pull the ball carrier's flag. The simplicity of the snap-to-flag dynamic keeps the game flowing without the chaos of tackling. It also teaches players awareness, timing, and reaction; skills that apply far beyond the field.

The Line of Scrimmage

The **line of scrimmage** is one of the most important, yet misunderstood, concepts for new coaches and parents. It's an imaginary line that runs across the field from sideline to sideline, separating the offense from the defense before the play begins. No player can cross this line until the ball is snapped. This rule is all about fairness. It prevents early movement and keeps every play balanced.

Understanding this line helps kids learn spatial awareness. It's a physical representation of boundaries and respect, the idea that everyone starts equal until the game begins. If a defender crosses the line too early, it's offside; if an offensive player crosses it before the snap, it's a false start. In both cases, the play is stopped, and a small yardage penalty is assessed to keep teams accountable.

Flag Pulls and Tackles

The defining difference between tackle football and flag football is how a play ends. Instead of bringing the ball carrier to the ground, defenders must **pull a flag** from the belt attached to the ball carrier's waist. This motion replaces tackling and keeps the game safer and more inclusive.

A clean flag pull requires precision and control. Players must aim for the flag, not the body. This teaches coordination and restraint, qualities as valuable in life as in sports. If a defender grabs clothing, makes physical contact, or blocks the ball carrier's movement, it's called illegal contact, and the offense gains yards.

Flag football also discourages reckless aggression by enforcing rules like **no diving** or **leaping** to pull a flag. These prevent collisions and keep the focus on strategy rather than force. Each of these rules exists to protect players, promote fairness, and encourage skill development over size or strength.

The Completed Pass

A play continues until a flag is pulled, a ball hits the ground, or a player scores. A completed pass happens when a receiver catches the football before it touches the ground and maintains possession. In youth leagues, the focus is on learning the fundamentals rather than enforcing strict professional-level rules, such as toe taps or forward progress. Most leagues consider a catch valid as long as the player has control of the ball with at least one foot, if not both, is inside the field of play.

Incomplete passes stop the clock and reset the down, teaching players about second chances and quick recovery. Interceptions, when a defensive player catches the ball intended for the offense, often result in an immediate change of possession. These moments build excitement and teach young players about transitions, situational awareness, and defensive instincts.

So essentially, every one of these basic rules, from how a play starts, what the line of scrimmage represents, how a flag pull works, and what defines a completed pass serves a greater purpose. They teach structure, patience, and respect for boundaries. When players learn to wait for the snap, stay behind the line, and aim for flags instead of bodies, they're not just learning a sport; they're learning discipline and sportsmanship.

For coaches and parents, understanding these fundamentals transforms how they communicate during games. Instead of frustration or confusion, they can explain the flow with calm confidence. It builds trust between adults and kids and creates an environment where everyone learns together.

By demystifying these basics, the field stops being a confusing patch of cones and whistles and becomes what it was meant to be, which is a place where clarity, teamwork, and joy collide.

CLARIFYING THE FLOW OF THE GAME: FROM KICKOFF TO FINAL WHISTLE

Once the foundational rules are understood, the next step is to see how the entire game unfolds from start to finish. Every youth flag football match follows a rhythm, a sequence of possessions, plays, and transitions that turn scattered movements into structure. When coaches, players, and parents understand this flow, the game stops feeling random and starts feeling intentional.

Opening Possession: Each game begins with an opening possession, which determines which team starts with the ball. In most leagues, this is decided by a coin toss, though some recreational divisions use a simple rotation system or let one team start the first half and the other start the second. The team that wins the toss chooses whether to start on offense or defense, and which direction they want to play. This early choice might seem small, but it shapes the strategy for the first series of plays. Flag football doesn't include traditional kickoffs, since removing high-speed collisions is part of what makes the game safer. Instead, play begins with the ball placed at a designated starting line, often the team's own 5- or 10-yard line. From there, the offense begins its drive, and the tone of the game is set.

The Drive and Downs System: Each possession is called a drive, and during that drive, the offense has a set number of downs (plays) to move the ball across a certain distance, usually to the midline of the field. Most leagues use a four-down system, meaning the offense has four attempts to reach either midfield or the end zone, depending on league rules. If they succeed, they earn another set of downs and continue their drive. If not, the ball changes possession, giving the opposing team their chance to score. This downs system teaches strategic thinking. Kids learn to balance risk and reward; when to throw deep and when to make a short, safe play. Coaches also learn how to manage momentum and adapt their tactics. For younger players, understanding that "you get four tries to move the ball" keeps things simple while teaching accountability: every play counts.

Turnovers and Possession Changes: When the defense gains control of the ball, it's called a turnover. This can happen through an interception (when the defense catches a pass) or when the offense fails to convert after their allotted downs. In some leagues, fumbles are considered dead balls, meaning the play ends where the ball hits the ground, while others allow the defense to recover it. Each variation exists to balance safety with learning opportunities. Turnovers are valuable teaching moments. They help players understand momentum shifts and resilience. A team that just lost possession learns how to reset quickly, while the opposing team gets a chance to capitalize. It's a real-world lesson in adapting after setbacks, a vital skill for both sports and life.

Scoring Plays: The objective of every drive is to reach the end zone, a rectangular scoring area at each end of the field. When a player carries or catches the ball in the end zone, it counts as a touchdown, worth six points. After scoring, the team attempts a conversion, which is a short play worth one or two extra points. Most leagues let teams choose between running or passing for one point from a shorter distance or attempting a longer play for two points. These options teach decision-making. Coaches can assess their team's confidence, skill level, or game situation to decide which conversion to attempt. For example, a team down by one point late in the game might go for two, showing kids how strategy and courage intertwine. Some leagues also recognize defensive scores, where a defender intercepts the ball and runs it back for a touchdown. While rare, these moments add energy and keep everyone engaged from whistle to whistle.

The Game Clock: Most youth flag football games are divided into two halves, each lasting anywhere from 10 to 25 minutes, depending on the age group and league format. Clocks typically run continuously except for timeouts, scores, or major stoppages. This running clock keeps the game flowing and reduces unnecessary delays. However, in the final minutes of each half, many leagues use a stop clock, pausing the timer after incomplete passes or after players go out of bounds, to ensure fair play in critical moments. Managing time teaches more than game awareness; it builds discipline and teamwork. Players learn how to hustle back to the line between plays, listen for signals, and operate under mild pressure. For coaches, mastering time management becomes a subtle art, balancing clock control with maintaining composure and readiness.

Ending the Game: When the final whistle blows, the game ends. But what happens if the score is tied? Different leagues handle this differently. Some allow ties, emphasizing sportsmanship and fun over competition. Others use overtime rules, where each team gets a single possession to score from a set distance. If one team succeeds and the other doesn't, the winner is declared. Overtime rules teach kids fairness and persistence, showing them that effort matters until the very last play.

In a nutshell, knowing the sequence from opening possession to final whistle changes everything. It allows coaches to anticipate, parents to follow along confidently, and players to understand where they are in the rhythm of the game. Instead of reacting blindly, they start playing with awareness. This awareness makes every play smoother, reduces confusion, and ensures that everyone on both sides of the ball can focus on what youth flag football is meant to be: a game that teaches structure, strategy, and joy all at once.

PENALTIES, FOULS, AND FAIR PLAY

Every sport needs a balance between freedom and fairness, and flag football is no exception. Rules protect the flow of the game and ensure competition stays friendly, not chaotic. Penalties aren't meant to punish but to keep the game safe, structured, and respectful for everyone on the field. When coaches, players, and parents understand why penalties exist, frustration gives way to understanding, and even a flagged play becomes an opportunity to teach discipline.

Common Penalties and What Triggers Them

Flag football removes physical tackling, but that doesn't mean it's a free-for-all. Here are the most common penalties you'll see in youth games and why they matter:

1. **Flag Guarding:** This happens when the ball carrier uses their hands, arms, or body to block a defender from reaching their flag. It's a natural instinct for kids to protect themselves, but this rule exists to prevent accidental collisions and keep defenders safe. When players learn to trust their speed and agility instead of shielding, they become sharper and more confident runners.

2. **Illegal Contact:** Any time a defender pushes, holds, or bumps a ball carrier instead of going directly for the flag, it's illegal contact. The same goes for offensive players who use their hands to push defenders out of the way. Flag football prioritizes space and control, so physical aggression is replaced by positioning and timing.
3. **Offsides and False Starts:** If a player crosses the line of scrimmage before the ball is snapped, play stops immediately. This rule reinforces discipline, teamwork, and patience; qualities that go beyond sports. It's also a great teaching tool for focus, as kids learn to listen for the snap instead of reacting too early.
4. **Illegal Forward Pass:** In flag football, the quarterback can only throw one forward pass per play, and it must occur behind the line of scrimmage. If they throw after crossing that line, the pass is illegal. This keeps plays structured and prevents confusion about ball movement.
5. **Too Many Players on the Field:** Each league has a set limit for how many players can participate in a play (often five to seven per team). Having extra players gives one side an unfair advantage. Coaches can use this rule to teach organization and awareness, making sure substitutions are managed carefully.
6. **Flag Falls Off Prematurely:** If a player's flag falls off without being pulled, the play is ruled dead when that player touches the ball. This avoids disputes about contact or intent and keeps the game flowing fairly.

Each of these penalties has one purpose: maintaining balance. They remind players that success comes from precision and teamwork, not shortcuts or aggression.

How a coach handles penalties can shape the entire tone of a game. When an official throws a flag, the best response isn't anger, it's curiosity. Instead of arguing, take a moment to ask what happened and then explain it to your players in plain language. For instance, here's a simple framework coaches can use:

"Here's what happened, here's why it's a penalty, and here's how we fix it."

That small moment of clarity turns a mistake into a learning opportunity. For example: *"We got called for flag guarding. That means we used our hands to block a flag. Next time, keep your hands up and just run. Trust your speed."*

This calm approach not only teaches the rule but models emotional control and sportsmanship. Parents, too, can adopt this mindset from the sidelines. When they understand the reason for a call, they can reinforce good habits rather than fuel frustration.

Promoting Fair Play and Respect

Flag football thrives when players understand that fairness isn't just about avoiding penalties, it's about how they carry themselves. Referees are there to protect the integrity of the game, not to control it. Coaches can encourage respect by teaching kids to self-report penalties, like stepping out of bounds or accidentally committing contact. This builds integrity and earns respect from both teammates and opponents.

Sportsmanship also extends beyond the whistle. Players should be taught to offer a hand to an opponent who falls, to high-five after tough plays, and to celebrate without taunting. These small gestures reinforce that competition and kindness can coexist.

Why Penalties Make the Game Better
At first glance, penalties might seem like interruptions. But in truth, they're part of what makes the game fair and fluid. They set boundaries that create creativity. When players know what they can and can't do, they start to explore new ways to succeed within those limits. That's where growth happens.

Every flag pulled, every whistle blown, every rule enforced contributes to a larger lesson: discipline, patience, humility, and respect. When those lessons take root, the field becomes more than a place to play. It becomes a classroom where fairness, confidence, and joy all play on the same team.

GLOSSARY OF KID-FRIENDLY FLAG FOOTBALL TERMS

Learning the language of the game helps everyone on the field speak the same way. For new players and parents, these words can sound like secret code at first, but once you know what they mean, everything starts to click. This glossary isn't just a list of terms; it's a translation guide that turns football talk into plain, fun language.

Snap

The snap starts every play. The player in the center passes the football backward, usually between their legs, to the quarterback to begin the action. Think of it as pressing the start button on a video game; it's the moment everything comes alive.

Line of Scrimmage

The line of scrimmage is an invisible line across the field where each play begins. No one can cross it until the ball is snapped. It's like a starting line in a race; everyone must stay behind it until the signal goes off.

Flag Pull

Instead of tackling, defenders end a play by pulling a flag from the belt of the ball carrier. This simple action replaces contact and keeps everyone safe. A clean flag pull is about timing and focus, not force.

Route

A route is the path a receiver runs to get open for a pass. It's like a planned dance move that tells the quarterback where to throw the ball. Common routes include slants, curls, and go routes, each designed to create space.

Blitz

A **blitz** is when a defensive player rushes the quarterback right after the snap. Most leagues limit how often this can happen to keep the game fair. It's a surprise move meant to pressure the offense, but only if done safely and by the rules.

Interception

An interception happens when a defensive player catches a pass intended for the offense. It's one of the most exciting plays in flag football, flipping possession in an instant and often leading to a score.

Huddle

The huddle is when a team gathers in a small circle before the play to discuss their plan. It's like a quick team meeting where players share the next move and build confidence before breaking out to the line.

End Zone

The end zone is the rectangular scoring area at each end of the field. When a player catches or carries the ball into the end zone, it's a touchdown worth six points. Think of it as the finish line where the celebration begins.

Conversion

After scoring a touchdown, a team gets a chance for a conversion, an extra play to earn one or two additional points. It's the flag football version of a bonus round; short, strategic, and often decisive.

Out of Bounds

When the ball or the player with the ball crosses the sideline, the play ends. This is called out of bounds. It teaches awareness and field control, reminding players to stay alert to their position on the field.

Rush Line

In most leagues, there's a rush line marked a few yards behind the line of scrimmage. Defenders who plan to blitz must start behind this line until the ball is snapped. It keeps plays fair by giving the quarterback time to react.

First Down

A first down is what a team earns when it reaches the yardage required to keep possession of the ball. It gives them a new set of plays (or downs) to continue their drive toward the end zone. It's a small victory inside the larger game.

Penalty Flag

When an official throws a yellow penalty flag, it means a rule has been broken. The play usually stops, and the ball moves forward or backward depending on the infraction. The flag is a reminder that fairness and safety always come first.

Possession

Possession simply means which team currently has the ball. Each side takes turns on offense and defense, teaching kids the rhythm of give-and-take that defines the flow of the game.

Audible

An audible is when the quarterback changes the play at the last second, usually after spotting something in the defense. It's a moment of quick thinking and teamwork. The quarterback might yell a word or number to signal the change, and everyone adjusts on the fly.

Fumble

A fumble occurs when a player accidentally drops the ball before the play is over. Depending on league rules, the ball is either dead on the spot or can be recovered by the defense. It's a lesson in focus and quick recovery.

Sportsmanship

Sportsmanship is the unspoken rule that matters most. It means playing fair, showing respect to referees, teammates, and opponents, and remembering that every player is there to learn and enjoy the game. After all, the best teams aren't just good, they're gracious.

These terms form the foundation of flag football language. The more kids, parents, and coaches use them, the smoother communication becomes. Before long, you'll hear players calling routes, parents cheering for first downs, and coaches using the right words to guide without confusion. That shared language is what turns a group of individuals into a real team.

QUICK-REFERENCE CHEAT SHEETS FOR GAME DAY

Even the best-prepared coaches and parents can get caught off guard on game day. Maybe a player forgets their flag belt, a parent questions a call, or no one can remember if it's third down or fourth. That's where certain reference guides come in to minimize that confusion. The following cheat sheets are designed to keep everyone on the same page when the clock is ticking and decisions matter.

Coach's Game Management Sheet

A simple, double-sided reference card can save an entire game from spiraling into disorder. Here's what every coach should have ready:

1. **Pre-Game Checklist**
   - Confirm all players have belts, flags, and mouthguards.
   - Check that cones, footballs, and pinnies are in place.
   - Review the lineup and rotation plan.
   - Confirm which direction your team is playing for the first half.

2. **In-Game Quick Rules**
   - Four downs to reach midfield, four more to score.
   - No contact, no blocking, no flag guarding.
   - Only one forward pass per play, behind the line of scrimmage.
   - A flag pull ends the play; diving or tackling is not allowed.

3. **Timeout Protocol**
   - Each team usually gets two timeouts per half.

- Use them for strategy, hydration, or calming momentum swings.
- Remind players that huddles should be quick and focused.

4. **Substitution Order**
   - Rotate every player evenly to keep participation fair.
   - Track playing time to ensure all kids get field experience.
   - Use a whiteboard or small roster card to check off substitutions.

Referee Signal Guide

For parents and new coaches, understanding referee gestures can make watching or managing a game far less stressful. Here are a few of the most common signals:

- **Arms folded:** Delay of the game.
- **One arm up and circling:** False start.
- **Hands on hips:** Offside.
- **Hands on top of head:** Illegal forward pass.
- **Arms extended forward:** Holding or illegal contact.
- **One arm swung downward:** Flag guarding or illegal block.

Knowing these signals lets coaches and parents respond constructively instead of arguing or guessing what just happened.

Quick Tips for Common Situations

Every game presents its share of unpredictable moments. These quick reactions can turn potential chaos into a smooth recovery:

- **If a player forgets their flag belt:** Sub them out immediately, and remind all players to double-check gear before every play.
- **If a parent questions a call:** Stay calm, acknowledge the concern, and refer them to the referee respectfully. Keep the focus on the kids.
- **If the rule is unclear:** Pause, breathe, and reference your league's printed rules or app version. When in doubt, prioritize safety and fairness over competition.
- **If a player gets frustrated:** Take a quick timeout. Use it to encourage, refocus, and model composure.

Parent Sideline Reference Card

Parents are part of the team environment, too. A small one-page sheet can help them support the game with confidence:

- **Key Reminders:** Cheer for effort, not just results. Respect officials and coaches. Keep feedback positive.
- **Top Rules to Remember:** No contact, flag guarding, or blocking. Touchdowns are worth six points; conversions add one or two points.
- **Game Flow:** Two halves, running clock, four downs per zone.

Cheat sheets help to stay composed under pressure. The best coaches and parents know that preparation builds peace.

When everyone understands the basics and respects the process, game day becomes smoother, safer, and more fun.

So print these, laminate them if you can, and keep them handy. When uncertainty hits, clarity will be in your pocket. That small bit of readiness can turn stressful moments into confident leadership, and that's how you set the tone for an unforgettable season.

Rules Build Freedom

Essentially, at the heart of every sport lies structure, and within that structure, freedom is born. The same is true for youth flag football. The rules we've explored in this chapter—including how a play begins, how it ends, what's allowed, and what isn't—aren't just boundaries. They're the framework that allows creativity, teamwork, and confidence to flourish.

When players understand the rules, they stop hesitating. The confusion disappears, and what replaces it is rhythm. You start to see the flow of the game, the coordination between a snap, a route, and a flag pull as a dance rather than a series of random motions. The whistle becomes a reset, not a reprimand. Every boundary creates an opportunity to think differently, to play smarter, and to find joy in precision.

For coaches, mastering the rules is an act of leadership. It allows you to teach with confidence, correct with kindness, and model calm under pressure. When a player looks to you after a call, your understanding becomes their reassurance. You're no longer just explaining football; you're teaching how structure leads to success. The coach who knows the rules well can turn every flag, every foul, every timeout into a teachable moment about patience and integrity.

Parents play a vital role, too. When they understand the flow of the game, they can support rather than question, encourage rather than criticize. The sidelines become a place of shared learning rather than a source of tension. Together, coaches and parents build a community where kids feel safe to make mistakes, learn, and grow.

And for the kids, the heartbeat of every field, these rules do more than shape how they play. They teach responsibility, respect, and resilience. They learn that fairness matters, that self-control is strength, and that boundaries don't limit greatness; they define it.

So the next time the whistle blows, listen closely. It's not just a sound that stops the game, it's a rhythm keeping everything in harmony because when everyone plays with clarity and respect for the rules, the field becomes more than a place for sport; it becomes a space where freedom, fun, and character all meet.

CHAPTER 5
PRACTICE LIKE A PRO- WINNING STRUCTURE FOR EVERY SESSION

The will to win is not nearly so important as the will to prepare to win.
— Vince Lombardi

Every great athlete, coach, or leader eventually discovers that success rarely comes from talent alone. It's the rhythm of preparation, the discipline of structure, and the consistency of effort that set great teams apart. Flag football is no different. The excitement of a touchdown, the precision of a flag pull, the energy of a well-timed play, all of it rests on what happens long before game day ever begins.

In the last chapter, we uncovered how understanding the rules brings confidence and freedom to both coaches and players. Once those foundations are clear, something new becomes possible: transformation through practice. Knowing the rules shows you what to do; structured preparation teaches you how to do it with excellence. This is where learning turns into mastery.

The beauty of flag football is that it rewards consistency more than chaos. A well-planned practice doesn't just keep kids busy, it builds habits that mirror real teamwork, decision-making, and trust. Every drill, rotation, and water break carries potential. With a clear structure, even a 60-minute session can develop not just skill, but character. Kids learn to focus, to persevere, and to understand that repetition is not boredom; it's how champions are made.

This is where coaches step into their most powerful role. Beyond calling plays or running drills, the coach becomes a builder of rhythm, turning scattered energy into momentum. With the right plan, practices stop feeling like time to fill and start becoming time to grow. That's the quiet secret behind every great season: the invisible hours that no one sees, shaping the visible moments everyone remembers.

Building Your First Practice: 60-Minute Plug-and-Play Plans by Age

Structure brings freedom. When a coach walks onto the field with a plan, everything changes: the kids stay engaged, transitions run smoothly, and the team leaves practice feeling like they actually learned something. The secret isn't having complicated drills or advanced plays; it's knowing how to use time wisely. Every minute counts, especially with young players whose attention spans can shift as quickly as a loose flag in the wind.

A strong practice has rhythm. It flows naturally from one activity to the next, striking a balance between fun and focus. Each session should be a well-paced story with a beginning that excites, a middle that challenges, and an ending that unites. Below are ready-to-use 60-minute practice templates designed for three key age groups. Each one emphasizes structure, simplicity, and repetition; the building blocks of confidence and growth.

Ages 6–8: Building Basics and Fun

Goal: Maintain high energy and keep learning light. Focus on basic movements, simple plays, and understanding how the game flows.

0–10 min – Dynamic Warm-Up

Use games like "Flag Tag" or "Sharks and Minnows." The aim is movement and laughter. Kids at this age learn best through play.

10–20 min – Core Skill Drill: Flag Pulling

Set up cones and have kids chase each other in pairs. Emphasize quick feet, safe space, and honest tagging. Reward clean pulls and sportsmanship.

20–35 min – Basic Offense Practice

Introduce simple routes: short slant, straight sprint, button hook. Keep it fun and rotate roles so everyone gets to throw, catch, and run.

35–50 min – Mini Scrimmage or Relay Game

Use half-field setups to keep kids active. Switch sides often to avoid fatigue. Make it competitive but light-hearted.

50–60 min – Cool-Down and Team Reflection

Circle up, stretch, and talk about one thing everyone learned today. End with a team cheer or fun question like, "What was your favorite play?"

Tip: Attention spans are short, so you may need to consider switching activities before kids lose focus. Use encouragement as your loudest whistle.

Ages 9–10: Sharpening Skills and Awareness

Goal: Balance skill-building with strategy. Start layering in positional understanding and teamwork.

0–10 min – Warm-Up and Reaction Drills

Use cone sprints, quick-feet ladders, or jump tag. End with a 30-second water break.

10–25 min – Core Offensive Skill

Work on catching mechanics and short passing. Pair players up, one throws, one catches, then switch. Keep the pace fast.

25–40 min – Defensive Focus: Flag Pulling + Positioning

Mark a small zone for defenders to protect. Teach angle pursuit and staying square. Praise awareness more than speed.

40–55 min – Controlled Scrimmage

Limit plays to 3–5 per drive. Encourage communication ("I got left," "Short route"). Stop mid-play to explain smart decisions.

55–60 min – Reflection and Stretch

Ask: "What worked well as a team?" "What will we try next week?"

Tip: Start giving short leadership moments; let one player call the team huddle or choose the next drill.

Ages 11–12: Game IQ and Team Identity

Goal: Introduce a structure that feels more like real football. Teach players to think, adjust, and communicate.

0–10 min – Active Warm-Up and Team Challenge

Use short relays or agility cone circuits. Add mini-competitions to keep intensity high.

10–20 min – Offensive Install: Plays in Motion

Run two or three base plays repeatedly. Teach timing and spacing. Rotate quarterbacks and receivers often.

20–35 min – Defensive Strategy: Zone vs. Man

Explain the difference, then demonstrate with short reps. Emphasize awareness of space over chasing the ball.

35–50 min – Live Scrimmage (Half Field)

Simulate real-game drives. Keep score, manage downs, and emphasize clock awareness. Encourage quick resets between plays.

50–60 min – Cool-Down + Team Debrief

Stretch, breathe, and recap. Ask players to name one thing they improved and one teammate who showed effort.

Tip: Kids this age crave responsibility, so give them ownership. Let them run warm-ups or suggest plays for the scrimmage.

A good practice plan doesn't just fill an hour; it sets a tone. Each session is an opportunity to teach rhythm, respect, and readiness. When time is structured with care, kids walk off the field tired, smiling, and proud, and that's when you know the work was worth it.

Warm-Ups and Cool-Downs That Kids Love

Preparation doesn't start with the whistle; it begins the moment kids step onto the field. A good warm-up awakens the body, focuses the mind, and builds excitement for what's ahead. For young players, it's the bridge between school-day energy and game-day focus. It turns chaos into readiness.

A proper warm-up raises heart rate, improves coordination, and primes muscles for motion. Furthermore, it establishes rhythm. Studies in youth athletics have shown that kids who start practices with structured movement retain focus longer and experience fewer injuries (Chapman, n.d.). Beyond the physical, warm-ups also set a tone: teamwork, listening, and shared momentum.

The best warm-ups feel like games. Instead of drills that feel like chores, choose activities that trigger laughter and movement at once. The goal is to engage both body and brain, creating a mindset that says, *'I'm ready to play.'*

Fun and Effective Warm-Up Ideas

1. **Flag Tag Frenzy (5–7 minutes)**

    Scatter cones across the field. Give each player a flag belt. The goal is to pull as many flags as possible in the time limit. Once a flag is pulled, players jog to the sideline, replace it, and rejoin the game. Keeps heart rates up and reflexes sharp.

2. **Sharks and Minnows (6 minutes)**

   Classic for a reason. Start with one or two *"sharks"* in the middle of the field and everyone else as *"minnows."* Minnows try to cross without losing their flag. Those who lose become sharks. Perfect for teaching evasion, awareness, and quick reactions.

3. **Cone Dash Challenge (5 minutes)**

   Set cones in a zigzag pattern. Players sprint through the course, practicing cuts and quick stops. Add variations like "reverse run" or "shuffle side-to-side." Make it competitive but upbeat.

4. **Pass-and-Go Relay (7 minutes)**

   Divide players into two teams. Each must pass the ball down the line and sprint to the back after their turn. Encourages teamwork, communication, and quick decision-making.

5. **Follow the Leader Dynamic Stretch (5 minutes)**

   Line up in rows. A coach or player leads stretches and movements: high knees, butt kicks, and arm circles. Let kids take turns leading; it boosts confidence and attention.

Cooling Down the Right Way

Just as a warm-up wakes the body, a cool-down teaches it to recover. It's more than stretching, it's reflection. The goal is to slow breathing, loosen muscles, and create a moment of gratitude and team bonding.

1. **Team Stretch Circle (5 minutes)**
   Form a circle, take a knee, and stretch together. Encourage slow, deep breathing. Let kids name one thing they learned or enjoyed about practice.
2. **Best Play Shout-Out (3 minutes)**
   Each player names one great play or teammate moment they noticed. Builds encouragement and highlights teamwork over competition.
3. **Mindful Breathing (2 minutes)**
   Have players lie on their backs or sit cross-legged. Guide them to take deep breaths, counting slowly to three. Helps regulate heart rate and reinforce calm.
4. **Victory Lap Cool-Down (4 minutes)**
   Jog one lap as a team, then walk one together. Finish with a team chant or *"hands in"* huddle to close the session with unity.

A good warm-up sharpens the body; a good cool-down strengthens the bond. When coaches treat both as essential instead of optional, kids learn that preparation and recovery are part of excellence. They begin to see that greatness isn't built only in the big plays, but in the quiet discipline before and after them.

KEEPING EVERY KID MOVING: ROTATIONS, STATIONS, AND SMALL GROUPS.

If you've ever watched a youth practice from the sidelines, you've probably seen one kid sprinting through a drill while six others stand waiting, eyes wandering, energy fading. The longer they wait, the less they learn. Flag football practices should pulse with motion. Every child should feel part of the action because movement is the heartbeat of engagement.

The best coaches aren't the ones with the loudest voices or the most complicated plays; they're the ones who master flow. They understand that attention and learning are directly tied to activity. When players keep moving, they stay alert, burn energy productively, and absorb lessons faster. The challenge, then, is not just running drills but designing an environment that makes stillness almost impossible.

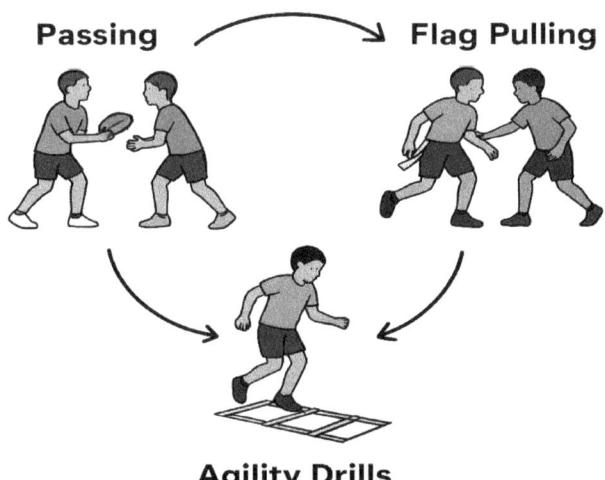

Diagram showing three-station rotation: passing, flag pulling, and agility drills

Step 1: Plan Your Stations

Choose three core skills to focus on: one offensive, one defensive, and one agility-based. For example:
- **Station 1:** Quick Passing and Catching
- **Station 2:** Flag Pulling and Evasion
- **Station 3:** Agility Ladder or Cone Footwork

Step 2: Divide and Conquer

Split players into small groups (3–5 per station). Assign one assistant coach, parent volunteer, or even a confident player to help lead each area.

Step 3: Keep the Clock Visible

Use a stopwatch or phone timer. Give each station 6–8 minutes before rotating. A short whistle signals the switch. Fast transitions build rhythm and responsibility.

Step 4: Debrief Between Rotations

After each full cycle, gather players for a quick, 1-minute review: "What did you learn? What can we do faster next time?" Small reflections turn repetition into mastery.

Tip: If you don't have helpers, run two stations and alternate your focus between them. While one group practices, the other watches or sets up the next activity.

Making It Engaging for Every Player

Kids thrive on variety. Mixing challenge and play keeps spirits high and learning natural. Introduce games into drills: turn flag-pulling into mini competitions, or time-based drills to see how many completions a group can make in 30 seconds.

Use color-coded cones or wristbands to form balanced groups. Shuffle teams mid-practice so players learn to work with everyone, not just their best friends. This avoids cliques and teaches adaptability, an underrated skill in both sports and life.

You can also build "activity ladders" to let kids advance at their own pace. For example, in a passing station:
- Level 1: Catch from 5 yards away.
- Level 2: Catch while moving.
- Level 3: Catch on the run and turn upfield.

Small, visible goals motivate kids and help them measure progress.

Sample Rotation Layouts

For 12 Players (3 Stations)
- 3 groups of 4 players.
- Each group rotates every 7 minutes.
- 1-minute breaks for hydration.

For 8 Players (2 Stations)
- Divide into 2 groups of 4.
- Alternate between flag-pulling and passing drills.
- Combine at the end for a mini scrimmage.

For 6 Players (Buddy System)
- Pair players as partners.

- Each pair alternates as offense/defense in mini-games.
- Rotate partners every 10 minutes for variety.

When every child moves, the practice becomes music: fast, coordinated, and full of joy. The field turns into a space where no one is left out, and every player's energy contributes to the whole. A coach who masters movement doesn't just teach flag football; they teach rhythm, teamwork, and the quiet confidence that comes from never standing still.

WHAT TO DO WHEN HALF THE TEAM SHOWS UP

Every coach eventually faces it. The sun is shining, the cones are out, the practice plan is perfect, and only four players walk onto the field. It happens more often than anyone admits. Between schoolwork, family commitments, and the occasional flu bug, attendance can be unpredictable. The key is not frustration but flexibility. The best coaches can turn a small turnout into one of the most productive sessions of the season.

The Power of Adaptability

A flexible coach doesn't panic when numbers are low, but they pivot. They understand that fewer players simply means more touches, more personalized instruction, and more leadership opportunities. Smaller groups can actually accelerate development because every player gets more reps, feedback, and time to experiment without pressure.

Think of it this way: full attendance teaches teamwork; low attendance teaches independence. Both are valuable. The art of coaching is learning to see potential in every situation.

Building Your Backup Plan

Preparation is freedom. Before the season begins, design two alternate practice templates:

1. Small Group Plan (3–5 Players)

Focus on fundamentals and versatility. Combine drills that keep everyone involved at once:

- **Passing Carousel:** One quarterback, two receivers, one defender. Rotate roles after each rep.
- **Flag Pull Gauntlet:** Set up a narrow lane with cones. One player runs through while the others practice clean flag pulls.
- **Mini Game to 3 Points:** Play half-field, offense versus defense. Switch sides after each score.

2. Compact Team Plan (6–8 Players)

You have enough for structure, but not full scrimmages. Try:

- **3-on-3 Drills:** Focus on timing and spacing.
- **Defensive Rotations:** Practice communication between safeties and rushers.
- **Relay Challenges:** Add competitive elements—flag pulls for speed, short sprints, or passing accuracy contests.

Tip: Keep a small whiteboard with quick setups drawn in advance. Visual cues help you pivot instantly.

Turning Short Numbers into Growth Moments

Low turnout days are perfect for individual development. Instead of cramming a normal practice into fewer players, shift the focus:

- **Skill Deep-Dives:** Spend time correcting technique, throwing form, catching grip, pursuit angles.
- **Leadership Opportunities:** Assign older or more experienced players to lead stretches or design a drill. This builds confidence and accountability.
- **Film or Chalk Talk:** If weather or space is an issue, move the group indoors. Watch short game clips or discuss real scenarios on a whiteboard. Teaching football IQ is as valuable as running drills.

Keeping the Energy Alive

Even with fewer players, energy must stay high. Use mini-competitions to maintain excitement:

- **Beat the Coach:** Players try to outscore or outlast you in quick drills.
- **Accuracy Challenges:** See who can hit a target or complete the most passes in 60 seconds.
- **Flag Frenzy:** Set a timer and see how many clean flag pulls can be made as a team.

Remember, small practices can strengthen team culture. They give coaches a chance to connect with players individually, encourage those who might usually blend into the crowd, and create memories that stick. When those players return to full-team sessions, they bring sharper skills and renewed confidence.

Quick Adjustments for Common Scenarios

If it starts raining: Switch to indoor drills, strategy talks, stretching, or simple bodyweight agility work.

If players are tired or distracted: Shorten drills and rotate faster. Engagement beats endurance.

If equipment is limited: Simplify drills. One football can run multiple games if organized well.

If energy dips: Call a quick team challenge or relay race. Competition always lifts spirits.

Every coach loves a perfect practice, but true coaching shows when things aren't perfect. Adaptable leaders teach their teams that consistency isn't about how many people show up; it's about showing up with purpose. A flexible plan is a sign of strength, and kids who see calm leadership under pressure learn that preparation and poise are the real victories.

Attendance Hacks and Motivating Consistent Participation

Now, a great practice plan means little if half the team doesn't show up. Attendance is the foundation of development. Without it, growth happens unevenly, chemistry weakens, and momentum fades. However, the truth is, most absences aren't caused by laziness. They happen because life for kids and families is busy, unpredictable, and sometimes overwhelming. The key isn't demanding perfection; it's building consistency through connection, communication, and motivation.

Creating a System That Works

Coaches who manage attendance well do more than send reminders; they create a structure that makes showing up easy. Start by establishing clear, reliable communication channels with parents and players.

1. Set Up Simple Communication Tools
- Use free apps like TeamSnap, WhatsApp, or GroupMe to keep everyone updated.
- Send short reminders a day before practice with details like time, location, and what to bring.
- Pin the season schedule at the top of the chat for quick access.

2. Create a Consistent Routine
When practice happens on the same days and times each week, attendance naturally improves. Predictability helps parents plan ahead and teaches kids responsibility. If the schedule must change, communicate early and clearly.

3. Designate a Parent Captain
Choose a reliable parent volunteer to help track attendance and send last-minute updates. Shared responsibility lightens your load and keeps everyone accountable.

Making Practice Worth Showing Up For

Kids show up for what excites them. A great coach doesn't just run practices; they create experiences that players look forward to. The more creative and connected the environment, the higher the turnout.

1. Add Theme Days
Simple themes make practice fun and memorable:
- *Superhero Day:* Wear shirts or flags in your favorite hero colors.
- *Crazy Socks Friday:* Small, silly traditions bring big smiles.
- *Challenge Day:* Compete in fun skill contests with mini prizes.

2. Celebrate Effort, Not Just Skill
Highlight hustle and teamwork over touchdowns. Give small weekly awards, like "Best Teammate," "Most Improved," or "Leadership Star." Recognition makes kids feel seen, and motivation follows naturally.

3. Use Team Rituals to Build Anticipation
Start every practice with a short team chant or end with a signature "hands in" call. Consistent rituals create a sense of belonging, and that sense of belonging drives attendance.

4. Keep Practices Fresh
Introduce a new drill or challenge each week. Even five minutes of something unexpected, like a "Beat the Coach" contest, keeps players curious and engaged.

Building a Culture of Commitment

Attendance improves when kids feel they matter. The culture you create as a coach determines whether showing up feels like a duty or a joy.

1. Make Every Player Feel Needed

Give each player a role in practice. Even if someone is injured or late, find a way to involve them. It could perhaps be as a timekeeper, assistant coach, or sideline motivator. Nobody should feel replaceable.

2. Involve Parents as Partners

Rotate small roles among parents; snack duty, water setup, or equipment help. When parents feel invested, their kids naturally follow.

3. Encourage Honest Conversations

If a player misses multiple practices, reach out gently. Ask if something's wrong, not just why they weren't there. Empathy strengthens commitment more than criticism ever could.

Handling Chronic Absences Gracefully

Not every attendance issue is simple, but patience and communication go a long way.

- **Send a Friendly Check-In:** A short text like, "We missed you at practice today! Hope everything's okay. Can't wait to see you next time," shows care without pressure.

- **Offer Make-Up Opportunities:** Share a short list of drills or challenges players can do at home. A five-minute flag pull or passing routine helps them stay connected.
- **Reward Return, Not Punish Absence:** When someone comes back after missing time, celebrate it. Encouragement rebuilds momentum faster than guilt.

Consistency is contagious. When one player shows up eager and ready, others follow. A coach's energy, structure, and care set the tone. When kids know their presence matters, they'll keep showing up not just for the game, but for each other.

Structure That Inspires Growth

Every field, every team, and every whistle blown is built on rhythm. From the warm-up to the final high-five, what separates a fun season from a forgettable one isn't talent but structure. When practices have flow, when kids understand the purpose behind every drill, and when coaches show up prepared, the field transforms into a classroom of life skills. That's where discipline, teamwork, and joy meet.

Coaches, your structure is your message. Every organized rotation, every consistent schedule, every encouraging word says something powerful: that showing up matters, that effort counts, and that growth is something we build together. Players see this long before they master a play. They sense it in your tone, in your timing, and in the way you handle chaos calmly.

A practice is more than a collection of drills; it's a story. Each session should tell players: *You belong here. You have a role. You are improving.* When that message becomes clear, attendance stops being a battle and becomes a habit. That's when learning takes root.

Quick Prompts for Coaches to Reflect or Try Next Week:
- What part of your practice gets the kids most excited, and how can you build on it?
- Can you trim five minutes of downtime by tightening transitions or adding a short mini-game?
- How do you recognize effort *(not just skill)* during each session?
- What's one creative theme or ritual you could introduce next practice to spark energy?

Recommended Practice Experiments:
- **The 10-Minute Challenge:** End practice with a surprise challenge, for instance, who can complete five perfect flag pulls or ten clean catches in ten minutes? Make it playful and build anticipation.
- **The Buddy Boost:** Pair a veteran player with a newer one for a short skill station. Encourage mentorship and confidence.
- **Mini Film Review:** Take two minutes after a scrimmage to highlight a smart play or decision. Kids love seeing learning celebrated in real time.

Remember, every coach starts as a planner, but the best ones evolve into architects of experience. The field becomes their blueprint, the drills their tools, and the laughter of their players the soundtrack of success. Preparation creates consistency, and consistency builds character. When your players learn to show up with focus, joy, and heart, they're not just practicing football, they're practicing life.

CHAPTER 6:
CORE SKILLS: DRILLS FOR EVERY AGE AND ABILITY

It's the little details that are vital. Little things make big things happen.
— John Wooden

Every great player, team, and coach eventually learns this truth: mastery resides in the details. Big wins are born from small movements repeated with focus and purpose. In flag football, the fundamentals are everything. The stance, the grip, the step, the pull—every motion builds a foundation that shapes the rest of the game.

Previously, we explored how structure and consistency create rhythm on the field, laying a foundation for us to take that rhythm and fill it with skill. These are the actions that turn structure into strength and repetition into growth. A well-run practice gives kids direction, but it's these core skills that give them confidence. The more they learn to move with purpose, the more the game opens up before them.

Think of a team like a living organism where every player is a moving part, every skill a heartbeat. When the basics are taught with patience and joy, those parts start to sync. A young player who learns how to pull a flag cleanly, catch a pass with focus, or change direction smoothly begins to experience something deeper than just play. They discover control, awareness, and pride in their own progress.

Every action is relevant. Drills and skills unlock potential, one repetition at a time. Whether a player is shy, fearless, fast, or still finding their rhythm, every skill taught with care becomes a seed for confidence, and once that confidence takes root, the rest of the game begins to bloom.

FLAG PULLING 101 — TECHNIQUES, GAMES, AND FIXES FOR COMMON MISTAKES

Flag pulling might look simple from the sidelines, but it's one of the most defining skills in youth flag football. Every great defensive play starts with a clean pull. It's where awareness, timing, and control come together in a moment that can change a game. Teaching kids how to pull flags properly builds not just defensive instincts, but also discipline, patience, and respect for the non-contact nature of the sport.

The Art of the Pull

Flag pulling is about precision, not aggression. It teaches young players that defense isn't about overpowering someone but outsmarting them. A clean pull shows self-control, quick reaction, and focus, qualities that build true confidence on the field.

The Stance: Begin balanced, feet shoulder-width apart, knees bent, and weight slightly forward. Encourage players to stay light on their toes, ready to move in any direction. The body should feel alive, not rigid, so reactions come naturally.

Eyes on the Hips: Players often chase what they see, the football, the arms, the face. But the hips never lie. Train kids to keep their eyes low and follow the movement of the hips where the flags hang. This focus improves timing and reduces missed pulls.

The Hands: Teach calm hands. The best flag pullers don't swing wildly; they reach with purpose. Both hands should move in, grab near the top of the flag strap, and pull straight down. Practice this slowly at first until it feels smooth and automatic.

Movement and Balance: Avoid lunging or diving. Instead, the player must shuffle their feet quickly, keeping their chest up and their arms ready. The player should glide rather than leap. This maintains control and prevents unnecessary collisions.

Finish Strong: After a pull, players should immediately stop, return the flag to their opponent, and reset. It's a small act of sportsmanship that builds mutual respect and keeps the energy of the game positive.

Building Skill Through Play

Drills should never feel like chores. Kids absorb technique best when it's disguised as fun, fast-paced competition. Below are activities that teach mechanics while keeping the laughter alive.

Flag Grab Relay: Players line up in a single file. The first player sprints five yards, grabs a flag from a cone or teammate, then races back to tag the next player. The goal is smooth, controlled motion, quick but accurate.

Mirror Tag: Two players face each other in a small square. One leads with side steps, fakes, and cuts while the other mirrors, waiting for the right moment to pull the flag. It trains patience, reaction, and spatial awareness.

Sharks and Minnows: A timeless favorite. One or two sharks start in the center while the minnows try to cross without losing their flags. When tagged, they join the sharks. It's fast, chaotic, and excellent for teaching pursuit angles and anticipation.

Flag Pull King or Queen: Set a timer for sixty seconds. Players move freely in a confined area, collecting as many flags as possible. The player with the most at the end wins. It sharpens reflexes and builds excitement.

Fixing Common Mistakes

Lunging Too Early: Teach the "breakdown" stance; knees bent, hips low, short, quick steps. Have players practice shuffling back and forth to build stability and patience before the pull.

Grabbing Jerseys or Arms: Use clear, visual cues during drills. Tell players, "See the flag, grab the flag." Colored targets help train eyes to focus where they should.

Losing Focus After a Missed Pull: Reinforce a short memory. Every missed flag is another chance to improve. Use quick resets and encourage a "next play" mindset.

Turning Technique into Team Energy

Flag pulling isn't just a skill, it's a rhythm the whole team can feel. Create challenges that spark excitement and unity.

The Flag Gauntlet: Set up a narrow lane of defenders. One player tries to sprint through without losing a flag. Switch roles every few turns. It's thrilling, fast, and teaches controlled pursuit.

Team Challenge: Split players into small groups. See which group can make the most clean pulls in two minutes. Reward teamwork and communication as much as results.

A perfect flag pull is like catching lightning in your hands—fast, focused, and satisfying. It's more than stopping a play; it's learning to stay calm under pressure and move with purpose. When kids master this balance of control and creativity, they begin to understand the deeper rhythm of flag football: precision over power, awareness over aggression, and joy in every clean pull.

Passing and Catching

Every highlight reel in football begins with the same two movements: a pass and a catch. These are the building blocks of connection, trust, and teamwork. In youth flag football, teaching passing and catching is less about strength and more about rhythm; how the body flows together in one smooth motion. A well-thrown ball builds confidence, but a well-caught one builds joy.

Teaching the Throw

Start with the basics: grip, stance, and release. Show players how to hold the football with their fingertips, not their palms, keeping a small space between the ball and their hand. The index finger should rest near the tip, giving them better control. Feet should be shoulder-width apart, front foot pointing toward the target, knees slightly bent. The motion should feel like skipping a stone—smooth, quick, and controlled.

Encourage them to step forward as they throw, using their legs for power rather than just their arms. For younger kids, lighter youth-sized footballs make all the difference. Remind them that accuracy matters more than distance. A perfect spiral isn't born overnight; it's shaped by patience and repetition.

Teaching the Catch

Catching is where fear often meets excitement. The key is to make it safe, fun, and repeatable. Start small. Use soft footballs, foam balls, or even beanbags to build confidence. Once players get used to the motion, transition to real footballs.

Teach the "diamond hands" position; thumbs and index fingers forming a triangle for chest-level passes. For lower or side throws, hands turn inward to guide the ball in. The moment the ball touches the hands, kids should tuck it close to their chest and turn slightly away from defenders. This habit protects the ball and prepares them for game play.

Drills That Build Rhythm

Partner Pass Challenge: Pair players up and count how many successful throws and catches they can make in one minute. Encourage them to beat their own record each round.

Moving Target Drill: Set up cones or hoops as targets. Award points for accuracy rather than distance. Helps players visualize throwing lanes and control their power.

Catch and Drop: Toss a soft ball, and after the catch, have players drop it immediately. This trains quick hand-eye coordination and timing without overthinking.

Station Throwing: Create throwing stations with different distances or targets. Players rotate every few minutes, building adaptability and endurance.

Common Challenges and Fixes

Alligator Arms or Flinching: Start close with slow tosses. Remind players to keep their eyes on the ball and their hands out. Gradually increase distance and speed as comfort grows.

Overthrowing: Have players focus on aiming rather than strength. Use a simple cue: "throw through, not over." Controlled follow-through leads to better accuracy.

Dropped Passes: Praise effort first. Use short, soft passes and remind them that misses are part of the learning process. Their goal should be consistency, not perfection.

Keeping Practice Fun

Kids love competition when it feels like play. End each passing session with short games that make them laugh and learn.

Quickfire Throws: Line up players and see who can complete three accurate passes in a row. Fast-paced and exciting.

Catch Relay: Divide into teams. Each successful catch allows the next player to go. The first team to finish the sequence wins.

Precision Circle: Players form a circle around the coach. The ball moves around quickly: catch, pass, move. It builds focus and reaction speed.

Overall, passing and catching teach more than motion; they teach trust. Every throw is an invitation, and every catch is a promise kept. When kids learn to connect through the ball, they begin to feel the heartbeat of the game: communication, timing, and the shared joy of making something work together.

Running Routes — Building the Route Tree with Visual Cues

Every good passing play begins long before the ball leaves the quarterback's hand. It starts in the mind of a receiver who knows exactly where to go, how to turn, and when to be there. Running routes is about timing, awareness, and rhythm; the unspoken language between passer and receiver. Teaching kids to run routes well means teaching them to move with intelligence, not just speed.

The route tree is the map of a receiver's world. Each branch, slant, out, curl, post, and go represents a pathway that helps the offense find space and create opportunity. Instead of overwhelming young players with terminology, introduce routes gradually, using visuals and physical examples. Draw them on the field with cones or chalk, or use laminated cards with pictures so they can see what they're about to do before trying it.

Start simple with four foundational routes:

- **Slant:** A quick diagonal cut across the middle: great for short passes.
- **Out:** Run forward, then cut sharply toward the sideline.
- **Go:** Sprint straight downfield at full speed: used for deep passes.
- **Post:** Run forward, then angle toward the center of the field.

Each route teaches a different skill: change of direction, acceleration, and body control. Once mastered, kids can start combining routes and understanding how spacing works in real plays.

Teaching the Movement

Start slow. Have players walk through routes first to understand the turns and timing. Use verbal cues like "plant and push" or "look early." Once they're comfortable, let them run at half speed, then full speed. Emphasize the importance of sharp cuts, balance, and keeping their heads up to locate the ball.

Follow the Leader: The coach or a confident player runs a route slowly while others mimic each movement. It helps visual learners and reinforces footwork and timing.

Simon Says Route Tree: Turn learning into a game. Call out routes, and players must react quickly and run the right pattern. It builds focus and memory through fun repetition.

Visual Learning Tools

Kids learn best when they can see their progress. Use cones, colored markers, or even tape on the ground to trace out each route. Assign colors to each route type: red for slants, blue for outs, yellow for posts, green for goes. Over time, kids will start to associate colors with movement, helping them memorize patterns faster.

Introduce laminated "route cards" that show a diagram of each route. Have players draw their own versions before practice, or have them review them in pairs. This makes the learning process more interactive and cements understanding.

Building Confidence and Game Sense

Once players understand routes individually, it's time to show how they fit into a team concept. Pair receivers to run complementary routes that create space for each other, like a slant and an out crossing paths. Explain that football is a puzzle, and routes are the pieces that fit together to create opportunity.

Encourage players to recognize defensive positioning. Ask simple reflective questions: "If the defender is close, where's the space?" or "How can you adjust your route to get open?" These teach decision-making beyond memorization.

Drills for Precision and Memory

Route Race: Divide players into groups. Call out a route, and see which group can execute it fastest and most accurately. Reward both speed and form.

Color Code Challenge: Place colored cones to mark routes. Players must run the correct route for each color called out by the coach. Tests both reaction time and memory.

Shadow Routes: Have one player act as the defender without grabbing flags. The receiver must complete their route cleanly while staying balanced and focused.

Adapting for Different Ages

Younger players may need shorter routes with fewer sharp turns. Keep explanations short, use visuals, and praise effort. Older players can handle more complex combinations and timing drills, including fake routes and quick breaks. Encourage creativity at every level. Let kids design a new route and name it. This builds ownership and enthusiasm. When they start imagining plays, they're not just following instructions anymore; they're thinking like football players.

So running routes is more than learning patterns; it's learning how to think on your feet. Each step teaches anticipation, patience, and trust. When a young receiver finds the perfect rhythm between mind, movement, and ball, that's when the game truly opens up before them.

As receivers learn to find rhythm in their routes, the natural flow of offense continues into another essential movement: the hand-off. If passing is about trust between two players separated by distance, hand-offs are about trust in proximity. It's the moment when teammates share the same space, timing, and heartbeat. Teaching safe, confident exchanges transforms hesitation into harmony and chaos into control.

SAFE HAND-OFFS AND LATERAL PITCHES FOR YOUNG PLAYERS

A clean hand-off starts with clear communication and steady body control. The quarterback and the runner must move like gears in a machine, each knowing what comes next without guessing.

Position and Posture: The runner approaches with arms in a "breadbasket" shape, with the inside arm up and the outside arm down, forming a pocket for the ball. The quarterback's motion should be smooth and deliberate, placing the ball firmly into that pocket without jamming or tossing.

Communication: Every hand-off begins with a cue. Simple words like "ready," "go," or "take" prevent confusion. In youth flag football, where contact and collisions are minimized, this clarity is vital for safety.

Timing and Motion: Encourage players to match speed during the exchange. The runner shouldn't slow down too early, and the quarterback should complete the motion before letting go. Practice at walking pace first, then at jogging speed, and finally at game tempo.

Teaching Through Repetition

Repetition builds rhythm. Start with drills that focus solely on coordination before adding defenders or pressure.

Hand-Off Alley: Players form two lines and practice running through a "lane" while exchanging the ball. Coaches can gradually add cones or obstacles to simulate movement under pressure.

Shadow Handoff: Without using a ball, have pairs mime the exchange repeatedly, focusing only on hand position, timing, and communication. It's an easy warm-up for beginners.

Add the Defender: Once players show confidence, introduce a passive defender. The goal is to maintain form while staying calm.

The Lateral Pitch

A lateral pitch feels flashier but should never be reckless. In flag football, it's often the difference between an extended play and a turnover. Safety and control must always come first.

Mechanics: The passer holds the ball with both hands, steps toward the receiver, and extends their arms outward, releasing the ball with a gentle flick. No overhand throws, no spins, just a smooth side toss that travels flat and short.

Eyes and Communication: The player receiving the pitch should keep eyes locked on the ball the entire time, hands open, and knees slightly bent. Encourage a short verbal cue ("now" or "yours") to ensure both players are synced.

Progression: Begin stationary, practicing the pitch at close range. Gradually add motion; first walking, then jogging. Avoid sprint-level drills until both players show consistent control.

Common Mistakes and Fixes

Dropped Hand-Offs: Remind players that slow is smooth, and smooth becomes fast. Rushing the exchange often causes fumbles. Have them take a deep breath before each rep.

Miscommunication: Use one consistent cue word per team. Mixing terms creates confusion during games. Keep it simple and repetitive.

Collisions: Teach spacing. The quarterback should step slightly aside after the exchange, and the runner should continue on their path without cutting too sharply. Small positional awareness prevents accidental contact.

Turning Technique into Flow

Once kids grasp the fundamentals, introduce real-time scenarios that link hand-offs and pitches into offensive plays. Combine them with route running or flag-pulling simulations to create a game-like rhythm. When players see how these skills connect, they begin to anticipate movement before it happens.

Mini Option Drill: Set up a quarterback, a running back, and a cone representing a defender. The quarterback decides whether to hand off or pitch based on the defender's position. This teaches awareness and adaptability.

Chain Reaction Drill: Have groups perform a sequence: short pass, hand-off, lateral pitch, then reset. The pace keeps players alert and reinforces transitions between skills.

A perfect hand-off or pitch isn't just a transfer of the ball, it's a transfer of trust. It teaches young athletes how to move in sync, read timing, and depend on their teammates. When done right, it feels effortless, almost like music; two players moving as one in the rhythm of the game.

Agility and Footwork - Fun Drills for Speed, Balance, and Body Control

After mastering hand-offs and pitches, players begin to understand that football isn't just about strength or strategy; it's about movement. Agility and footwork are what give young athletes control over their bodies, helping them change direction, dodge defenders, and move confidently across the field. When coached with creativity and fun, agility training becomes one of the most exciting parts of practice.

Why Agility Matters

Agility isn't just quickness, it's coordination, balance, and awareness. Every flag pull, every cut, and every route depends on a player's ability to move efficiently. In youth flag football, agility also helps prevent injuries by teaching kids to stop safely, pivot under control, and stay balanced even when they're off-balance.

Explain to players that being agile means being adaptable. The goal is to teach their bodies to react with purpose, not panic.

Warm-Up and Foundation Drills

Start with movements that prepare muscles and joints for action. Short, playful warm-ups help players stay loose and energized.

Cone Shuffle: Line up five cones about three feet apart. Players shuffle side to side through them, keeping knees bent and eyes forward. This builds lateral quickness and foot coordination.

Zig-Zag Race: Set up cones in a zig-zag pattern. Players weave through them while maintaining control of their speed. You can turn it into a relay for extra excitement.

Hop Ladder: Use chalk or rope to create a ladder on the ground. Players hop through the spaces first with both feet, then alternating feet. This simple exercise sharpens rhythm and balance.

Building Coordination and Reaction

Once players are warmed up, transition to drills that engage their minds as well as their feet.

Mirror Drill: Pair players up. One player leads with quick foot movements while the other mirrors every motion. Switch roles every 20 seconds. This teaches reaction and focus.

Shadow Tag: Without contact, players chase each other within a small boundary, trying to match steps without stepping out of bounds. Great for developing field awareness and body control.

Reaction Cone Drill: Place cones of different colors in random order. Call out a color, and players must sprint to touch the correct one. This improves decision-making speed and acceleration.

Combining Agility with Game Skills

Agility shouldn't exist in isolation. Integrate it with flag-pulling, route running, and defensive positioning to make it feel game-real.

Flag and Dash: Players sprint five yards, then quickly change direction to pull a flag from a partner. It links quick movement to defensive skill.

Route and React: Have players run a short route, stop instantly on command, then accelerate again. This mimics real in-game cuts and reactions.

360 Awareness Drill: Players stand in the center of a cone circle. On the coach's call, they must sprint to a random cone and back, turning sharply each time. It builds spatial awareness and explosive turning ability.

Making It Fun for All Ages

Younger kids thrive on imagination. Rename drills to make them playful:

- **Lightning Feet:** quick side shuffles with cheering for speed.
- **Stealth Ninjas:** balance challenges that test stillness after sudden movement.
- **Capture the Cone:** competitive races that mix agility with teamwork.

Older players can handle more structured challenges, like timed obstacle runs or agility ladders with ball-handling components. Track their progress over time to build motivation and show improvement.

Encouraging Growth and Confidence

Always celebrate effort before speed. Agility drills can feel frustrating for kids who struggle with coordination, so coaches should focus on encouragement rather than perfection. Phrases like "quicker every time" or "you're moving smoother now" reinforce growth.

Incorporate reflection moments. After drills, ask players what movements felt easiest and what challenged them. This builds self-awareness and helps them take ownership of their improvement.

Agility is the heartbeat of football in general. It's the invisible skill that makes every play look smooth, and every effort look easy. When kids master their movement, they don't just play the game better; they move through it with confidence, control, and joy.

DRILLS FOR SHY OR LESS ATHLETIC KIDS - CONFIDENCE-BUILDING ACTIVITIES

Every team has that one player who stands at the edge of the group with their hands behind their back, eyes down, quietly waiting to be noticed. Maybe they've never played before, maybe they've been laughed at, or maybe they just haven't found their voice yet. For them, football isn't just a sport; it's an emotional mountain. The goal of this section isn't to make them faster or stronger right away; it's to help them feel seen, safe, and capable.

Confidence isn't built by drills alone; it grows when someone believes in you. Coaches and parents play a vital role here. A quiet word of encouragement, a simple "I'm proud of you," or a smile when a child finally catches that pass can shift an entire mindset. Many professional athletes once struggled with shyness. Michael Jordan was famously cut from his high school basketball team. Lionel Messi barely spoke as a child, often described as reserved and introverted. Yet what helped them rise wasn't instant talent; it was consistency, encouragement, and people who didn't give up on them.

When working with shy or less athletic kids, slow down the pace. Focus on participation and connection rather than performance. Let them succeed in small ways first, for instance, catching one pass, pulling one flag, or giving one good effort. Each win, no matter how small, builds the foundation for the next.

Creating Safe and Supportive Spaces

Start every session by setting the emotional tone. Remind the team that everyone learns differently, and effort matters more than speed. Pair quieter kids with patient teammates who naturally encourage rather than compete. The goal is to create safety before skill.

Confidence Circle: Begin practice with a quick group check-in. Ask each player to share something they liked about the last session. It builds camaraderie and lets every voice be heard, even briefly.

Partner Uplift Drill: Pair players. After a short exercise, such as a pass or a flag pull, each partner must give one piece of positive feedback. This simple activity shifts the culture toward mutual encouragement.

Personal Best Tracker: Instead of comparing players, help them track their own progress. A shy child who improves their catching success from one out of five to three out of five should feel just as celebrated as the star player scoring touchdowns.

Drills that Build Comfort and Fun

The key is to create motion without pressure through activities that get kids laughing, moving, and realizing they belong.

High-Five Relay: Every player who completes a run or catch earns a high-five from the coach or team. It's small, but touch and affirmation matter deeply to shy kids.

Catch and Clap: Players catch a soft ball, then clap their hands to celebrate. The sound is an instant confidence booster, a physical reminder of success.

Flag Tag Lite: Play without winners or losers. The goal is simple movement and fun. For beginners, this breaks the fear of "messing up."

Encouraging Parents to Join the Process

Furthermore, parents can unknowingly add pressure when all they mean to do is help. Encourage them to focus on emotional support instead of correction. When a child looks to the sideline, they shouldn't see disappointment; they should see belief.

Share this simple reminder with parents: *"Your child will remember your tone longer than the score."* Encourage post-practice conversations that start with, "What did you enjoy?" rather than, "What did you do wrong?"

Coaching the Heart, Not Just the Player

Some kids don't need louder voices; they need quieter confidence. A coach who kneels to eye level, listens, and gives specific praise can transform a player's experience. Instead of "good job," say, "I like how you stayed focused on that flag," or "That was brave, nice effort." Precision in encouragement builds identity. Remember that not every child will love competition right away. For some, the first victory is just showing up. Others may bloom later, long after the season ends. The job of a good coach is to plant seeds that last.

Sports often reflect life. A shy child learning to run without fear learns something far deeper than football; they learn that mistakes aren't final, and courage can grow with every try. It's not just their body that's getting stronger; it's their sense of worth.

As they laugh during a relay, celebrate a catch, or cheer for someone else's success, confidence begins to take root. One day, they won't need reminders to speak up or step forward. They'll just do it because someone once gave them space to grow.

When a child who once hid behind the line finally raises their hand to volunteer for a drill, that's the real touchdown. It's a quiet kind of victory that echoes long after the whistle blows.

Key Takeaways - Building Skill, Spirit, and Confidence

1. **Skill and safety grow together.** Every drill, from flag pulling to agility, should teach kids how to move with purpose and control. Confidence follows structure.

2. **Progress beats perfection.** Celebrate small improvements as loudly as big wins. For young players, one successful catch or clean hand-off can change how they see themselves.
3. **Coaching is leadership through care.** The best coaches teach technique, but the great ones teach belief. A few sincere words can turn fear into courage.
4. **Agility is more than speed.** It's the art of balance: physical, emotional, and mental. Helping kids find rhythm in their movement gives them rhythm in their confidence.
5. **Create safe spaces.** Before a child can perform, they must feel accepted. Building trust on the field builds trust in themselves.
6. **Parents are partners, not pressure.** Encourage them to value joy, effort, and attitude over outcomes. The echo of encouragement lasts far longer than any score.
7. **Every player has a story.** Some are loud, some are quiet, but all deserve to be seen. The heart of youth coaching lies in finding each child's spark and helping it shine.

Ultimately, football, at its best, is a classroom for life. Each skill learned, each fear faced, and each word of encouragement exchanged shapes not just players, but people. The wins will fade, but the confidence built here will certainly last a lifetime.

CHAPTER 7:
MANAGING PEOPLE: COMMUNICATION, PARENTING, AND TEAM CULTURE

People don't care how much you know until they know how much you care.
- Theodore Roosevelt

Every great team begins not with the perfect playbook, but with the right connection. You can teach drills, explain rules, and draw routes all day long, but until your players trust you, they won't truly listen. Until parents see that your goal is to help their kids grow, not just win games, they won't fully buy in. And until everyone, from the shyest six-year-old to the loudest sideline dad, feels they have a voice and a place, the team will only ever function at half its potential.

So now we're stepping beyond cones and flags into conversations, encouragement, correction, and community. It's where leadership gets tested in the real world, not through game scores, but through tone, empathy, and patience. Managing people in youth flag football means managing personalities, emotions, expectations, and relationships, all while keeping the laughter alive and the lessons meaningful.

Earlier, we built your foundation: understanding the game, its benefits, the rules, the plays, and the drills. Now, we build the team culture that makes all of that come alive. Here, we learn how to talk so kids understand, how to listen so parents feel valued, and how to respond when frustration or conflict sneaks in. Because no matter how many diagrams you draw, it's your communication that will determine whether this season runs smoothly or falls apart.

Managing people requires a certain level of connection to them. It's about learning to speak a language that motivates them instead of intimidating them. It's remaining calm in the midst of chaos, bringing humor to tension, and bringing purpose to every conversation. In this chapter, we'll walk through eight key areas where that leadership comes to life, from explaining drills in kids language, to handling sideline coaching, to celebrating effort the right way.

So, take a deep breath. The whistle's in your hand. Let's talk about how to lead not just a team, but a family of growing players who will remember how you made them *feel* long after they forget how to run a post route.

CLEAR COMMUNICATION

Communication is the heartbeat of coaching. It shapes how players understand, how parents perceive, and how the entire team environment feels. Before a whistle ever blows, communication sets the tone. Good communication doesn't begin with shouting directions from the sideline; it starts with clarity, empathy, and presence. The coach who can simplify complexity, listen actively, and adjust their words to match who they're speaking to is the one who creates growth that lasts beyond the game.

In youth flag football, every word matters. A child's mind processes language differently depending on their age, confidence level, and even how their day went before practice. The best coaches recognize this and meet players where they are. They understand that saying less can sometimes mean saying more, and that how something is said often matters more than what is said. It's not just instruction, it's translation, turning football into kid language.

Let's picture a moment on the field. The coach gathers the players around to teach a route. Instead of saying, "You'll run a five-yard out from the slot position," he crouches to their level and says, "Okay, team, imagine you're running straight to the mailbox, then boom, turn and run to the sidewalk. That's your path." Immediately, heads nod. Kids smile because they get it. The game becomes familiar, even fun.

Simple analogies turn confusion into confidence. Use comparisons kids understand, such as video games, races, treasure hunts, or everyday objects like cones as 'checkpoints.' When explaining defense, you might say, "Your flag is your treasure. Protect it. Keep your eyes on anyone who tries to steal it." It paints a picture that sticks, and kids remember it because they feel it.

Clarity also grows through demonstration. Some kids learn by seeing, others by doing. Mix verbal instructions with visuals. Show the route. Walk it out. Let the kids act it out. If a drill involves spacing, lay down cones to mark where they should stand. Color-code where possible. For auditory learners, repeat key terms rhythmically: "Run, plant, turn, catch!" The repetition helps ideas stick and keeps energy high.

When you notice confusion, pause. Ask questions like, "Who can show me how that looks?" or "Can someone explain it in their own words?" These small moments turn learning into dialog, not a monologue. They help you spot who's lost without embarrassing them. If kids seem unsure, use a 'thumbs up or sideways' check before moving on. It's a quiet, quick way to gauge understanding while keeping the momentum.

Tone is just as important as words. A calm, encouraging tone draws attention better than a loud correction. A coach who smiles while speaking builds trust. Instead of saying, "Don't drop the ball," try, "Let's see how many we can catch in a row." The brain responds to positive phrasing by focusing on what to do instead of what not to do. Over time, this rewires how kids process instruction and builds confidence from within.

Communication also happens beyond the whistle, for instance, eye contact, posture, and patience say more than a long speech. For instance, a coach who kneels to speak to a child at their level shows respect. A high-five after effort shows that trying matters. Even silence can be powerful when used well. A moment of pause before feedback shows thoughtfulness and invites reflection.

For coaches, developing good communication is a lifelong skill. Practice it. Reflect on it. After each session, ask yourself:

- Did I make things clear?
- Did I listen as much as I spoke?
- Did I help every player feel seen?

These small reflections shape growth over time. A great communicator doesn't just teach the game; they teach kids how to understand themselves, their teammates, and how to work together.

So when you walk onto the field next, remember that clarity breeds confidence, and confidence breeds connection. Speak with purpose, teach with imagination, and listen like it matters, because to every child out there, it truly does.

DEALING WITH SIDELINE COACHING AND OVER-INVOLVED PARENTS

Every coach will face it at some point: the parent who can't stay silent during practice or game day. You'll hear it from the sidelines: "Run left! Pull the flag! Throw it sooner!" While the intentions are good, the effect on the team can be confusing, discouraging, and disruptive. Kids freeze, unsure of whose voice to follow. The coach's authority weakens, and the joyful rhythm of learning gets replaced by pressure.

Sideline coaching rarely comes from malice; it comes from love and excitement. Parents want their children to succeed, and in the rush of emotion, they start calling plays from the stands. The goal isn't to shame or silence them but to guide their enthusiasm into the right channels. The best coaches manage this with grace, clear expectations, and proactive communication.

Start by setting the tone early. Before the first practice, hold a brief parent huddle. Smile, thank them for showing up, and say something like:

"I'm grateful for every parent here. We all want these kids to have fun, learn, and grow. To make that happen, we'll keep one voice giving instructions during practice and games: mine. That helps the kids stay focused and confident. If you'd like to help, we'll have plenty of ways to get involved off the field."

A calm, inclusive tone defuses tension before it ever begins. When expectations are clear from day one, you rarely have to address problems later. If a parent forgets and starts coaching mid-game, handle it privately after the play. Avoid confrontation in front of others. A quick, respectful conversation might sound like this:

"Hey, I really appreciate how engaged you are. It's awesome seeing your passion. Just remember, we agreed on one voice for instructions. It helps the kids stay focused. If you'd like, I can send you our practice plan, so you know what we're working on this week."

That approach validates their involvement while gently steering them back to boundaries. You're not fighting a parent; you're inviting them into partnership. Sometimes that single private chat is all it takes.

You can also prevent sideline stress by giving parents healthy roles that redirect energy. Assign someone to be the team photographer, snack coordinator, or carpool organizer. Ask for volunteers to help with setup or post-game clean-up. The more ownership parents have, the less likely they are to overstep. They feel included, not excluded.

Still, there may be moments where emotions flare, especially during close games or tough calls. In those cases, the best response is composure. Keep your focus on the players, not the sidelines. Afterward, reach out to the parent with a calm message:

"I know everyone gets caught up in the moment; it's part of the fun. Let's both remember we're modeling sportsmanship for the kids. I want them to see how adults handle competition the right way."

Tone and timing make all the difference. Frustration handled publicly creates division; patience handled privately builds respect. Remember, parents aren't opponents; they're allies who sometimes need gentle redirection.

To reinforce your culture, include a one-page "Parent Code of Conduct" at the start of the season. Keep it simple and friendly with three or four bullet points that summarize the expectations: respect, positivity, and unified communication. Review it at your first meeting and reference it when needed.

A strong parent-coach partnership transforms everything. When parents trust you, the kids relax, teamwork blossoms, and game day feels like a community instead of a competition. Managing sideline coaching enhances unity between the coach, players, and parents. When everyone speaks with the same voice of encouragement, the field becomes a place where confidence grows louder than criticism.

PARENT ENGAGEMENT - SIMPLE WAYS TO GET FAMILIES INVOLVED

A youth flag football team isn't just made up of players and coaches; it's built on the support of families who show up, cheer, and make the experience richer for everyone. Parent engagement is more than just attendance; it's involvement that builds community. When parents feel part of the process, kids feel supported, coaches feel less overwhelmed, and the team develops a spirit that lasts long after the season ends.

The key is to keep it simple and intentional. Not every parent can commit large amounts of time, but nearly every parent can contribute something meaningful if given the right opportunity. The coach's job is to make involvement accessible and fun, not a burden.

Start with an invitation that sets a welcoming tone:

Coach says: "We're building a team where everyone has a role. Whether you can help once or every week, there's always a way to be part of what we're doing."

Provide a list of small, clear tasks that fit different personalities and schedules. For example:

- **Snack Coordinator:** Organize a simple rotation so kids have healthy snacks and water each game day.
- **Team Photographer:** Capture moments at games or practices for end-of-season highlights or a slideshow.
- **Carpool Organizer:** Help connect parents who can share rides, easing transportation stress.
- **Spirit Parent:** Lead cheers, bring music, or decorate banners to build excitement.

- **Equipment Helper:** Set up cones, distribute flags, and assist with cleanup after practice.

Each of these roles adds to the team's flow and reduces pressure on the coach. You can create a sign-up sheet, a group chat, or a quick online form where parents can volunteer. Many families appreciate being asked directly, so you can also approach them one-on-one:

Coach says: "You've got great energy out there. Would you be interested in leading our cheer group this weekend?"

Parent responds: "Sure, I can do that!"

Coach says: "Perfect. The kids will love it, and it helps us all stay fired up."

When parents see the immediate impact of their involvement, they're more likely to stay engaged. Be sure to publicly recognize their contributions; simple appreciation goes a long way. Try ideas like these:

- Shout-outs after games: "Let's give a round of applause for Mrs. Moyo for organizing snacks this week!"
- Small thank-you tokens: a team photo, a note signed by the kids, or a badge that says "Super Supporter."
- End-of-season appreciation event: a casual picnic or awards day where parents are celebrated alongside players.

Troubleshooting engagement is also part of the job. Some parents will be shy or unsure how to help; others may try to take over. To balance that, set expectations early. Let everyone know that participation is encouraged, but teamwork is key. Emphasize shared goals rather than personal agendas.

Coach says: "Every bit of help makes the team stronger. Just remember, we're all here to support the kids together, no job is too small."

Encourage open communication. Keep parents informed through weekly messages, short updates, or quick huddles after practice. It's not just about logistics; it's about connection. The more parents understand what's happening on the field, the more confident and cooperative they become.

Ultimately, when parents are engaged, the entire culture changes. Kids show up with pride because they feel the family energy around them. Coaches feel supported instead of stretched, and families begin to bond through these shared experiences. A youth flag football team becomes a small community where everyone, from player to parent, has a purpose.

As families begin to move in sync with the team's rhythm, another layer of growth emerges: the personal confidence of each player. This confidence isn't born of perfect games or flawless drills; it grows from how feedback is given. So now let's explore the art of using constructive feedback not just to correct, but also to build, strengthen, and inspire resilience in every child who steps onto the field.

CONSTRUCTIVE FEEDBACK - ENCOURAGEMENT THAT BUILDS CONFIDENCE

In youth sports, feedback is more than correction; it's coaching the heart as much as the skill. Every word you speak can either plant confidence or sow doubt. A well-timed compliment, a calm tone after a mistake, or a few encouraging words in front of the team can change how a young player sees themselves. Feedback is not about perfection; it's about direction.

The goal is to guide players toward growth without crushing their spirit. Kids interpret tone and body language faster than words. A coach who looks frustrated can discourage, even when saying the right thing. That's why constructive feedback begins with mindset: you're not fixing players, you're building them. The difference is subtle but powerful.

Start with observation. Watch how each player responds to pressure and success. Some thrive on public praise, others shrink from it. Some need gentle redirection, others respond to challenge. When you understand their personality, you can tailor your words so they land with meaning instead of noise.

For example:

Coach says: "That was a great route, and I love that you hustled even after the pass didn't connect. Let's work on your timing next round."

Player responds: "Got it, Coach."

Coach says: "Perfect. That kind of effort makes all the difference."

That short exchange does more than correct technique; it builds trust. The player knows they're seen, not just judged.

Use the "praise, suggestion, praise" model; it's simple but powerful. Start by affirming effort, then offer one clear adjustment, then end with encouragement. For example:

Coach says: "You were quick to the flag, nice work! Next time, keep your hips lower so you can move faster. You're really improving with each play."

This keeps kids listening because they feel supported, not scolded.

When addressing mistakes, stay calm and specific. Avoid general phrases like "You need to focus" or "You're not trying." Instead, pinpoint the behavior you want to change and explain why. For example:

Coach says: "Let's reset. Watch the quarterback's eyes before you move. That's your cue. You've got this."

Coach says: "Hey, that drop happens to everyone. What did you notice about your hands that time?"

These questions turn feedback into learning. They shift the focus from failure to problem-solving.

Create moments for group encouragement, too. After a tough play or loss, gather the team and emphasize effort over outcome.

Coach says: "That game was close. I'm proud of how everyone kept hustling until the whistle. We'll clean up the small stuff next time. What matters is that you didn't quit."

Positive reinforcement should always feel genuine. Kids can sense false praise instantly. Instead of saying, "Good job" after everything, focus on something real: "I saw how you kept your head up even after that missed pull." The details make the difference.

Remember that feedback isn't only verbal. A thumbs-up, nod, or high-five says just as much. Even a quiet acknowledgment after practice, a quick word like "You were locked in today, nice work," builds confidence over time.

For more reserved players, private encouragement is more effective than public praise. Pull them aside and say, "I can see how much effort you're putting in. Keep it up." They'll remember that moment long after the next game ends.

Constructive feedback turns mistakes into milestones. It helps kids learn resilience, responsibility, and self-belief. When they hear encouragement from you, they start speaking that same encouragement to themselves. That's how you build confidence that lasts beyond the field.

HANDLING DISCIPLINE AND DISAPPOINTMENT - GROWTH-MINDED RESPONSES

Every season brings its moments of frustration, tears, and tough calls. Whether it's a missed flag, an argument on the sideline, or a player who refuses to participate, how a coach handles those moments defines the team's culture. Discipline and disappointment are inevitable, but they don't have to damage morale. With the right approach, they become powerful opportunities for growth.

Kids are learning how to handle emotions they don't yet have words for. A good coach becomes both teacher and stabilizer, helping players turn setbacks into lessons. The first step is consistency. Rules and expectations should be clear from the start of the season. Create them together with the team, so players feel ownership. For example, you might say:

"Let's come up with our team rules. What kind of behavior helps us play our best? What makes practice fun and fair for everyone?"

When kids contribute, they're more likely to follow the rules because they helped create them. Post those agreements where everyone can see them or repeat them at the start of each practice.

When a player breaks a rule or gets upset, the coach's response should be calm, not reactive. Yelling or showing frustration usually makes things worse. Instead, use calm redirection.

"Take a quick breather. Let's cool off for a minute, then we'll try again."

or: "I can see you're frustrated. That's okay. We'll talk about what happened after practice."

This approach preserves dignity. It teaches self-control instead of shame. Discipline should always correct behavior without crushing confidence.

When dealing with disappointment, timing matters. After a tough loss or bad game, emotions run high. Avoid long speeches or lectures right away. Focus on effort and attitude.

Coach says: "That one was rough, I know. But I saw heart out there, and that's what counts. We'll go over the details tomorrow when everyone's fresh."

By separating the emotion from the correction, you help kids learn emotional balance. The next day, when everyone's calmer, revisit the moment as a learning opportunity.

Coach says: "Remember how that play felt yesterday? What could we try differently next time?"

Player responds: "Maybe I should've waited before pulling the flag."

Coach says: "Exactly. That's smart thinking. That's how you grow."

Always end discipline or correction with reconnection. A quick high-five, a smile, or a small word of affirmation lets the child know they're still valued.

Coach says: "You handled that better today. Proud of you for bouncing back."

Discipline is most effective when it feels fair and predictable. If rules change depending on your mood, kids will test limits. Stay steady, stay patient, and explain your reasoning when possible. This teaches accountability, not fear.

For example:

Coach says: "We sit out one play when we interrupt. That's a reminder to give others a turn. Once you're ready, you're right back in."

When disappointment runs deeper, like being benched, missing a play, or losing a big game, validate the feeling first.

Coach says: "It's okay to be upset. That just means you care. Let's figure out how to turn that into fuel for next time."

Empathy doesn't weaken discipline; it strengthens it. It reminds kids that correction comes from care. Every player will face hard moments, but how they're guided through them determines whether those moments leave a scar or build character. Great coaches don't avoid conflict or disappointment; they transform them. They show kids that growth isn't always comfortable, but it's always possible. And when kids see that even their mistakes have purpose, they learn to face challenges with courage instead of fear.

TEAMWORK, LEADERSHIP, AND SPORTSMANSHIP

A youth flag football team is more than a group of kids chasing a ball; it's a living classroom where teamwork, leadership, and sportsmanship become lessons for life. The game might end in twenty minutes, but what players learn about unity, empathy, and respect stays with them for years. We need to understand how these values grow through experience, how they shape identity, and how a coach can nurture them with purpose.

Teamwork

Teamwork is where kids first learn that success is rarely a solo act. It's easy to spot the talented player who wants to do everything alone, the one who believes scoring is the only way to win. But sooner or later, that player discovers that even the best run means nothing if no one's there to celebrate it with them.

Teamwork teaches kids the art of belonging. It's the understanding that every role matters, from the receiver who blocks, the teammate who cheers from the sideline, and the one who keeps morale high after a fumble. Each small contribution builds something larger than the individual.

When players work together, they learn patience, listening, and trust. They begin to understand that their teammate's success doesn't threaten their own; it strengthens it. The quietest child starts to feel confident, and the most confident one learns humility. You can see it happen during a drill when a child who once shouted, "I'll do it myself!" suddenly passes the ball and shouts, "Go, go, go!" That's growth in motion.

As a coach, foster that spirit through shared challenges. Try group drills that can't be completed unless every player participates. Set mini-goals that reward cooperation instead of competition. Encourage phrases like "We've got this" or "Let's try again" to replace "I messed up" or "That's your fault."

Beyond the field, teamwork becomes a mirror for life. In school, in families, and later in work, every child who learns to collaborate now will know how to connect later. The field becomes the first place they experience unity, not as a word, but as a heartbeat.

Leadership

Leadership is one of the most misunderstood concepts in youth sports. Many assume it means being in charge or being the best. True leadership, though, is about responsibility, not authority.

It's the ability to lift others, to stay steady when things fall apart, and to inspire through example.

Every child has leadership potential. Some show it loudly with words, others, quietly, with action. The coach's role is to draw it out. Give each player a chance to lead warm-ups, help explain a drill, or guide a teammate through a challenge. These moments plant seeds of confidence.

Leadership in life works the same way. Think of people like Nelson Mandela, who led with forgiveness; or Mother Teresa, who led through compassion. Their strength came from serving, not commanding. In sports, that translates to the player who encourages others after a mistake, helps a teammate up, or thanks the referee. Those small acts define real leadership.

Still, leadership isn't easy. It requires patience, consistency, and the humility to admit when you're wrong. For young players, that might mean learning to lead without bossing others around, or learning to stay calm when their teammates don't listen. Coaches can turn these moments into lessons by asking reflective questions like, "How did it feel when no one followed your lead?" and "What can we do differently next time?"

Celebrate leadership that serves the group, not just the scoreboard. When a child volunteers to help a nervous teammate or gives up their turn for someone else, highlight that behavior. Let the team see that leadership isn't about the spotlight, it's about selflessness.

Sportsmanship

Sportsmanship is where the heart of the game lives. It's how players handle victory and defeat, fairness and frustration. It's easy to be kind when you're winning, but real character shows up in how you respond when things go wrong.

Teaching sportsmanship starts with example. Kids are always watching how adults behave. If a coach argues with a referee, they'll remember it. If a parent cheers respectfully even when the team is losing, they'll remember that too. The field becomes a reflection of adult behavior long before it becomes a measure of athletic ability.

There will be moments when emotions run high, such as a bad call, a dropped flag, or a game lost by inches. Those are golden teaching opportunities. Instead of lecturing, pause and guide reflection. Ask, "What can we control right now?" or "How can we show respect even when we're upset?" The goal is to help kids understand that sportsmanship isn't just about rules, it's about who they're becoming.

Sometimes, the most powerful lessons come from loss. There's a story of a youth team that lost every game in their season but became the most admired team in the league. Why? Because they never stopped cheering for each other, never blamed, never quit. They clapped for opponents, celebrated small wins, and left every field with heads high. Those kids learned more about life than any trophy could teach.

Encourage sportsmanship through rituals. Have your team shake hands before and after games. Create a "Respect Circle" where players name one good thing about the opposing team. Make fairness part of your culture, not an afterthought.

When teamwork, leadership, and sportsmanship come together, you're not just coaching flag football, you're coaching life. The lessons learned here shape character beyond the field. Kids learn to lead without pride, to win without arrogance, and to lose without bitterness.

Years later, they may forget the scores, the drills, even the plays, but they'll remember the laughter, the encouragement, the sense of belonging. They'll remember the coach who believed in them, the teammate who passed the ball, and the feeling of being part of something bigger than themselves.

That's the victory that lasts.

HANDLING UPSETS, MISTAKES, AND DISAGREEMENTS

Every team, no matter how well-trained or well-spirited, will face moments that test its unity. A dropped catch in the final seconds, an argument between teammates, a game lost after a perfect week of practice—these are the moments that reveal what kind of environment you've built. Handling upsets, mistakes, and disagreements breeds understanding, resilience, and growth.

When emotions run high, the coach becomes the anchor. Kids look to you not just for instructions, but for tone. If you stay calm, they learn to be calm as well. Similarly, if you handle frustration with patience, they begin to mirror that patience in their own reactions. Every emotional storm is an unspoken lesson in composure.

The first thing to remember is that disappointment is not failure; it's feedback. Mistakes show where growth can happen, and disagreements show where communication needs strengthening. When a player makes a costly mistake and their shoulders slump, that's your moment to teach recovery. Walk over, give them space, and say something that helps them reset: "You're learning. Shake it off. Let's focus on the next play." That simple reassurance teaches that worth isn't tied to performance.

Sometimes, frustration takes a louder form. Two players might argue over a missed flag or a misread pass. Instead of rushing to discipline, guide them through reflection. Pull them aside and ask, "What happened?" Let each one speak without interruption. Then bring them back together and find common ground. Remind them, "You're on the same team. Every great team learns how to disagree without falling apart." This helps children understand that conflict is part of growth.

Create emotional routines that help your team reset after mistakes. Try the "Take a Breath" rule. Whenever a player gets frustrated, they step aside, take three deep breaths, and then rejoin play. It normalizes emotions instead of punishing them. Over time, they start doing it on their own without being told.

You can also use short reflection breaks after challenging plays. Ask simple questions like, "What worked that time?" or "What can we change next time?" The goal is to turn reactive energy into learning energy. When kids learn to reflect, they learn to adapt.

One of the hardest lessons to teach is that losing doesn't erase effort. After a tough loss, don't rush into analysis. Let the kids process first. Maybe they sit quietly, maybe they're teary-eyed, that's okay. Then, when the moment feels right, remind them of what matters most. Tell them how proud you are of their effort, their teamwork, and their heart. Let them see that a loss can still carry pride when it's met with dignity.

It's also important to model how adults handle mistakes. Admit your own when they happen. If you called the wrong play or forgot something during practice, own it openly. Say, "That one's on me, team. Let's fix it together." That honesty permits kids to be imperfect, too.

For disagreements that go deeper, like ongoing frustration between players, create time outside the game for resolution. Sit with them, not as a referee, but as a mentor. Help them express what they feel without blame. Sometimes just being heard softens the hardest hearts. End those talks with unity, maybe even a small handshake or gesture that says, "We move forward together."

Resilience is simply learning how to stand up again, not pretending everything's fine. The teams that grow strongest are the ones that learn how to rise together. When players begin to see mistakes as stepping stones and disagreements as doorways to deeper trust, they're no longer just athletes. They're growing into teammates, communicators, and leaders.

A season built on grace and growth will always outlast one built only on victories because long after the trophies gather dust, it's the lessons from the hard days, the missed catches, the heated moments, the tears turned into laughter that shape who these kids become.

Celebrating Effort, Progress, and Team Spirit

Growth doesn't always look like a win on the scoreboard. Sometimes it looks like a team walking off the field together after a loss, heads held high. It looks like the quiet kid finally calling for the ball, or the player who struggled for weeks finally pulling a flag cleanly. These moments are victories too, and they just don't come with a medal. They come with heart.

Celebration is the glue that keeps a team connected through the highs and lows. It reminds players that progress matters just as much as results, and that effort is something to be proud of. After all, it's easy to cheer when things go right; the real magic is cheering when growth is still in progress.

After a game or practice, take a few minutes to recognize effort out loud. It doesn't have to be formal. It could be as simple as, "I saw how you kept running even when you were tired," or "You didn't give up after that drop, and that's what champions do." When kids hear effort being celebrated, they start valuing it as much as performance.

You can make celebration a tradition. Some coaches create a "Player of the Day" moment, not necessarily for the best player, but for the one who showed hustle, teamwork, or a positive attitude. Others keep a jar filled with slips of paper where players write something great they noticed about a teammate; small acts of encouragement that turn into a culture of appreciation.

Find ways to make celebrations collective, rather than individual. After a tough drill, have the team huddle and share one thing they're proud of from that session. It might be a new skill, a moment of bravery, or simply showing up with a good attitude. These shared acknowledgements build connection and pride in the group.

Even parents can be part of it. Encourage them to highlight progress at home. A quick text to the coach or a word after practice like, "He's really enjoying being part of the team," reinforces the community spirit that youth sports are meant to build. Most importantly, keep the celebration authentic. Kids know when praise is real. A smile, a nod, a high-five, or a few sincere words can mean more than an elaborate ceremony.

In the end, celebration isn't just a response to effort; it's fuel for the next one. Every acknowledgment tells a child, "You matter. What you're doing matters." And when that message echoes through a team, something beautiful happens. The kids stop playing just to win; they start playing because they love the game, each other, and the journey they're on together.

That's how every great season ends, not precisely with a trophy raised, but with hearts full and spirits lifted, ready for whatever comes next.

Leading Beyond the Field

Every coach who steps onto the grass is building more than a team; they're shaping character, confidence, and community. The lessons in communication, teamwork, leadership, resilience, and celebration don't stop when the final whistle blows. They follow these kids into classrooms, friendships, and the rest of their lives. The true victory of a season isn't the scoreboard alone; it's the transformation that happens in every player who learns to believe, to listen, to lead, and to care.

So as you lead, remember that your voice carries weight far beyond the field. The tone you set today becomes the mindset they carry tomorrow. Teach with patience, correct with love, and celebrate with joy. That's what great coaching is: it's leadership wrapped in compassion.

Key Takeaways

- Communication builds clarity, trust, and connection. Speak with purpose and simplicity.
- Encourage parent involvement through clear boundaries and shared goals.
- Feedback should guide, not shame, praise effort, refine skill, and inspire confidence.
- Discipline is an opportunity to teach emotional control and accountability.
- Teamwork, leadership, and sportsmanship are the heartbeats of the game. Nurture them daily.
- Mistakes and disagreements are stepping stones; they grow character and resilience.
- Celebrate effort and progress consistently, creating a culture of appreciation and unity.

When the season ends, it's the relationships you built, the lessons you taught, and the young lives you helped shape that remain relevant, and that's the real championship.

CHAPTER 8:
TOOLS, RESOURCES, AND NEXT-LEVEL COACHING.

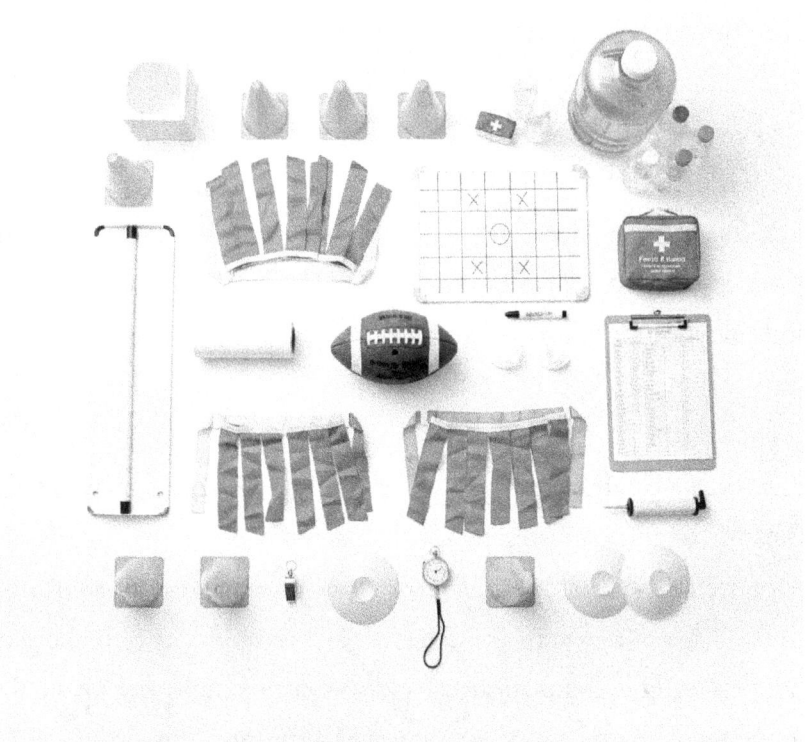

The moment the whistle blows on game day, the difference between a flustered sideline and a confident one often comes down to one thing—preparation. The best coaches don't just wing it; they build systems that make the chaos run smoothly. Practices feel organized, players know what's next, and parents understand their role without needing a crash course every week. That's the heartbeat of coaching at the next level: structure without stiffness, freedom within a plan.

Most youth coaches start with passion, and that's the right place to begin. But passion alone won't keep a practice running when ten kids need attention, one forgot their flag belt, and the clock's already ticking. That's where tools step in to your aid as quiet assistants, keeping everything in motion. A simple checklist, a clear rotation chart, and a set of printable practice plans; these turn good intentions into rhythm. They give you space to actually coach, not just constantly catch up.

Think of it as building your own management playbook. Just like players need a route to run, coaches need a route to lead. Every system you create, from the way you start warmups to how you handle post-game wrap-ups, builds consistency that kids thrive on. And consistency, more than complexity, is what turns a group of kids into a team.

So this is where we start streamlining the season: laying out the practical, coach-tested tools that make your practices flow, your games run smoother, and your parents feel part of the mission because when the logistics are handled, the magic can happen and the focus returns to what matters most: the joy of the game and the growth of every player who steps onto your field.

TOOLS AND RESOURCES FOR THE MODERN COACH

1. Printable Practice Plans

A well-structured practice is the foundation of every great team experience. Printable practice plans save time and mental energy. Each one is organized by **age group** and **duration** to match attention span and skill level.

Duration	Ideal Ages	Focus	Structure
60 Minutes	9–12	Full practice with drills and scrimmage	Warm-up (10m), Skill stations (20m), Team drills (20m), Cool down (10m)
45 Minutes	7-9	Core fundamentals	Warm-up (10m), Skill focus (15m), Game simulation (15m), Wrap-up (5m)
Rainy-Day 30 Minutes	All ages	Indoor or limited-space fun	Movement drills (10m), Passing games (10m), Mental warmups (10m)

Each template includes space for:
- **Attendance tracking**
- **Weekly focus points** (e.g., teamwork, flag pulling, passing)
- **Notes** for quick adjustments

Tip: Keep laminated copies in your coaching folder or use a dry-erase board version to adapt quickly on-field.

2. Pre- and Post-Practice Checklists

Checklists simplify chaos. They help new coaches remember every detail from equipment setup to end-of-day team talks.

Pre-Practice Checklist:
- Flags, cones, footballs, and belts packed
- Practice plan printed or opened on device
- Warm-up cones placed in formation
- Parent helpers assigned roles
- Team huddle theme ready (character word of the week)

Post-Practice Checklist:
- Collect equipment (check flags and belts)
- Reinforce one positive highlight per player
- Briefly address what's next (next practice or game)
- Team cheer wrap-up

Bonus Tip: Create a digital version in Google Sheets for assistants to update from their phones.

3. Game Day Organization Templates

Nothing kills momentum faster than sideline confusion. Game day templates bring structure to chaos.

Coach's Sideline Sheet

Player Name	Starting Position	Rotation #1	Rotation #2	Special Role
Example: Aiden	QB	WR	Safety	Captain

Substitution Tracker: ensures fair play time and keeps energy high.
- Use color codes (Green = on field, Yellow = next in, Red = resting)
- Update every quarter or series.

Pro Move: Keep laminated versions with erasable markers. Kids love seeing their name rotate into the lineup; it builds excitement and ownership.

4. Parent & Helper Role Assignments

Parents love to contribute when they know how. Clear roles remove confusion and strengthen the community.

Role	Responsibility	Rotation Example
Snack Parent	Bring halftime fruit and water	Rotate weekly
Equipment Helper	Set up cones, flags, and goals	2 parents per practice
Photographer	Capture highlight photos	1 volunteer per game

Tip: Post a simple rotation chart via group chat each week. The more parents feel involved, the stronger the culture becomes.

5. Cue Cards for Real Moments

In most cases, coaching is more about timing, tone, and composure. Keep cue cards handy for quick resets.

Coach's Calm Card

For stressful moments:

Breathe. Step back. Kneel to eye level. Ask: "What can we fix next play?"

End with encouragement. Never match emotion with emotion.

Sportsmanship Reminder Card

For team huddles:

"We play hard, we play fair, we celebrate others."

"Respect the whistle. Respect each other."

Tip: Print and laminate both cards. They work wonders for assistant coaches, too.

When tools like these become part of your rhythm, coaching shifts from reactive to proactive. You stop managing chaos and start mastering flow. Each resource, simple, structured, and field-tested, frees your focus for what really matters: connecting with your players and enjoying the game's spirit.

Game Day Preparation

The day the scoreboard lights up, and the field fills with noise, is when all the preparation pays off. Game day is now about executing what's already been built in practice. The goal is simple: smooth transitions, clear communication, and an atmosphere where every kid feels part of the action.

1. Pre-Game Flow

Game day begins long before the whistle. Small habits set the tone.

Coach's Pre-Game Routine:
- Arrive early (30–45 minutes before players). Walk the field, check for safety hazards, and mark boundaries.
- Layout cones and warm-up zones in advance.
- Review roster, rotations, and substitution plan.
- Have backup flags, belts, and one extra football ready.
- Greet each player with confidence; energy is contagious.

Team Warm-Up Sequence:

Step	Duration	Focus
Dynamic Stretching	5 Min	Loosen up muscles, build focus
Flag Pull Drills	5 Min	Sharpen reflexes, light competition
Passing Pairs	5 Min	Reconnect timing between QB and receivers
Walk-Through Plays	10 Min	Run 2–3 key plays at half speed

Tip: Keep warm-ups short and lively. Overcoaching before kickoff drains excitement, whereas energy should rise, not plateau.

2. Sideline Systems and Substitution Rhythm

A well-run sideline is like a calm cockpit; everyone knows their station.

Sideline Setup:
- Divide your sideline: one section for active players, another for *resting players*.
- Mark cones or tape to define zones. Visual order reduces chaos.
- Assign one assistant or parent to help manage rotations.

Substitution Rhythm:
- Plan rotations by time, not emotion. Set clear intervals (e.g., every 5 minutes or every two drives).
- Announce subs early so kids aren't surprised.
- Use hand signals or cards for substitutions instead of shouting across the field.

Pro Move: Keep a laminated rotation chart clipped to your clipboard. Kids respond better when they see their turn coming, instead of waiting in uncertainty.

Sample Substitution & Sideline Rotation Template

Player Name	Starting Position	Rotation 1	Rotation 2	Time On Field	Rest Time	Notes
Example: Aiden	QB	WR	Safety	5 Min	2 Min	Captain, leads huddle
Example: Liam	WR	RB	Rest	5 min	5 Min	Focus on catching drills next week
Example: Zoe	Defense	QB	WR	5 Min	3 Min	Rotate mid-game for balance

3. Communication During Play

Game day communication defines composure. Keep it short, calm, and clear.

Coach Talk Guidelines:
- One keyword or cue per play (e.g., "Protect," "Watch middle," "Stay home").
- Speak to players, not at them; eye contact makes direction personal.
- Celebrate effort loudly; correct mistakes quietly.

Huddle Consistency:
- Huddles should last under 10 seconds.
- Rotate who calls the chant, it gives ownership to players.

Tip: Use consistent phrasing week to week. Predictability in language builds confidence in young players.

4. Handling On-the-Fly Adjustments

Every game has surprises, for instance, the weather, mismatched skill levels, missing players, and many other factors. That's why adaptation is a skill of its own.

When Things Shift:
- Simplify. Drop complex plays and focus on one strong route combo.
- Rotate positions to challenge kids and cover absences.
- Shorten play calls and speed up tempo if energy dips.

In-Game Problem-Solving Mini-Guide:

Scenario	Response
Opponent dominates speed-wise	Focus on zone coverage, limit space
QB struggling with accuracy	Switch to short passes and handoffs
Low morale after turnovers	Call a timeout, celebrate small wins
Missing Key Player	Redistribute roles, simplify responsibilities

Tip: Maintain emotional control, as it can spread easily. Kids mirror your body language and tone faster than your words.

5. Post-Game Wrap-Up

The way a coach closes a game sets the emotional memory kids carry home.

Post-Game Routine:
- Gather players immediately after the handshake line.

- Acknowledge one team-wide success (e.g., defense effort, sportsmanship, energy).
- Highlight 2–3 individual efforts without making it about stats.
- Keep the tone celebratory even in the face of loss, then end with the team chant.
- Quick parent huddle: thank them, remind them of the next schedule, and dismiss everyone with clarity.

Pro Tip: Save detailed corrections for the next practice. The field after a game is for encouragement and unity.

Game days reveal who prepared, which reflects not just the players, but the coach as well. The systems you establish here turn long Saturdays into smooth, spirited experiences that parents appreciate and players remember. When every part of your day runs with rhythm, your team doesn't just play, they perform with purpose.

DIGITAL DIAGRAMS & VISUAL PLAYBOOKS

Before a whistle ever blows, kids learn faster when they see what they're about to do. Digital diagrams and visual playbooks turn confusing arrows and football jargon into something tangible; color, shape, and motion they can understand. This section helps you create, teach, and use digital visuals that simplify the game for every player, no matter their learning style.

1. Visual Playbooks

A visual playbook is the bridge between your strategy and a child's imagination.

Visual Playbooks work perfectly because:
- Kids are visual learners; they grasp patterns faster than verbal instructions.
- Colors, icons, and arrows make learning routes and positions memorable.
- It keeps parents engaged, and they can help reinforce plays at home.

How to Build One:

1. **Start with a Clean Field Template** – Use a simple editable field (see sample below). It should include zones, end zones, and faint yard markers.
2. **Add Player Icons** – Circles or avatars labeled QB, WR, RB, C, etc. Keep consistent colors (e.g., blue = offense, red = defense).
3. **Draw Movement Paths** – Use arrows for routes, dashed lines for passes, and solid lines for running paths.
4. **Add Visual Cues** – Cones, flags, or highlight zones where the play focuses.
5. **Keep Text Minimal** – Use short tags like "Quick Pass," "Fake," or "Pull Flag."

Tip: Consistency matters. Keep all plays in one color theme and symbol system so players recognize patterns instantly.

EDITABLE FIELD TEMPLATE:

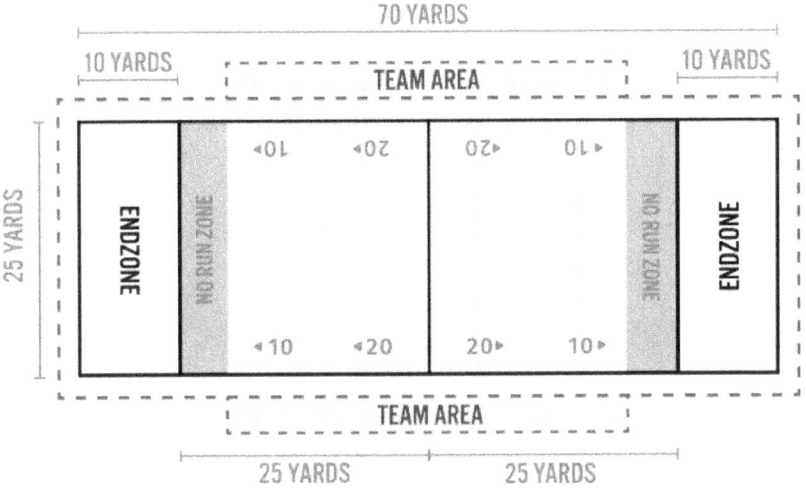

This field layout can be printed or edited digitally. Leave a blank space below for adding your own players, cones, or zones.

Mockup Description (for visual creation):
- Clean green turf background.
- Yard markers every 5 yards.
- Light grey outlines for boundaries.
- Offense/defense icons in simple circles with clear labels.
- Space for arrows and editable movement lines.

2. Sample Play Diagram - "Double Out" (Offense)

Below is a visual concept of one of the simplest yet most effective youth flag football plays. It teaches spacing, timing, and short route precision.

Play Breakdown:
- **Formation:** Two wide receivers (WRs), one center (C), one quarterback (QB), one running back (RB).
- **Motion:** Center snaps to QB, both WRs run short out routes (5 yards then turn), RB runs a short flare route for backup.
- **Goal:** Create quick open options and build passing rhythm.

SAMPLE PLAY DIAGRAM:

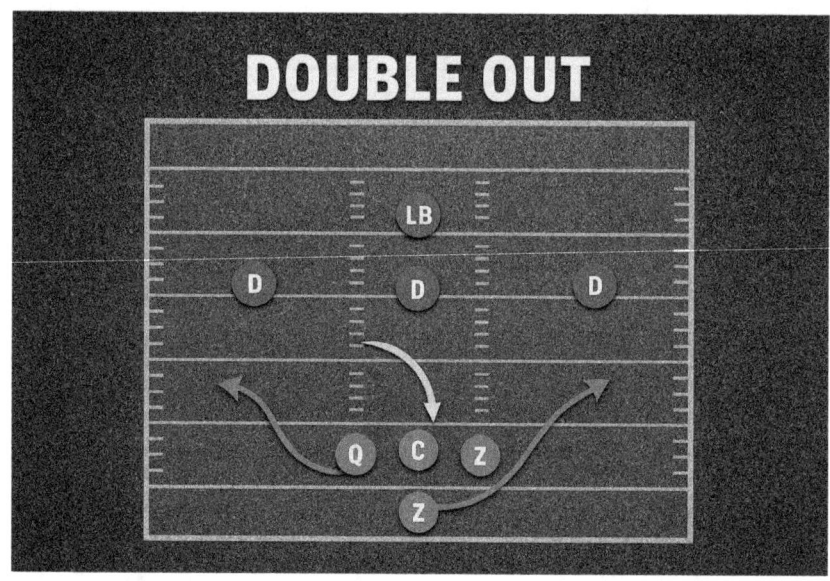

(Double Out" Play Visual)

Mockup Description (for visual creation):
- Green field background.
- Blue circles for offensive players.
- Solid blue arrows for receiver routes (angled outward).
- Dashed blue line from QB to receiver (showing pass).
- Yellow cone icons marking route depth.

Coach Tip: For young players, use physical cones on the field that match the diagram colors. It helps connect screen visuals to real field positions.

3. Tools for Creating Digital Diagrams

You don't need expensive software to make professional, easy-to-read visuals. Here are some accessible tools:

Tool	Platform	Ideal For	Cost
Canva	Web, Mobile	Quick templates, color coding, printables	Free / Pro plan
Playmaker X	Web, iPad	Full football diagram editor with animations	Free / Paid tiers
Coach D	iOS, Android	Youth-friendly drag-and-drop play creator	Free
PowerPoint / Google Slides	Desktop, Web	Simple diagram creation using shapes and arrows	Free
Sketchbook or Draw.io	Web	Customizable field and drill illustrations	Free

Pro Move: Save all plays as **image files (PNG or JPEG)** and organize them in a shared folder for assistants and parents.

4. Teaching with Diagrams

Once your visuals are built, how you present them matters even more.

Effective Presentation Flow:

1. **Show the Visual:** Hold up your tablet or printout and let them look first, but don't talk just yet.
2. **Name the Play:** Say the name once and point to the routes or arrows.

3. **Explain Simply:** Use child language, for example: "You run to the blue cone, then turn."
4. **Walk It Out:** Move to the field and recreate it physically.
5. **Reinforce It Digitally:** Send the visual home via parent group chat or team folder.

Tip: Always connect visuals to action. Kids remember *movement*, not speech.

5. Printable and Editable Templates

To make your playbook interactive, offer both print and digital resources. For instance, you can consider the following template suggestions:

- Blank Offensive & Defensive Field Sheet (PDF or Canva Link)
- Player Route Design Worksheet (kids can draw their own plays)
- Weekly Drill Diagram Sheet *(See template below)*

WEEKLY DRILL DIAGRAM SHEET

MONDAY	TUESDAY	WEDNESDAY	TURIDAY

FRIDAY	SATURDAY	

DRILL NAME	KEY NOTES

EQUIPMENT IEED	
DIAGRAM	

Weekly Drill Diagram Sheet Template

Play Notes Sheet – Coaching Reflections

This is designed to help coaches *track lessons, strategies, and observations* from each game or practice. It doubles as both a printable and digital template that's already clean, structured, and easy to reuse weekly. The purpose is to help coaches record what worked, what needs adjustment, and how individual players are developing. It's also a self-check tool for leadership, communication, and team growth.

Template Layout
Game / Practice Date
_____

Opponent / Focus Theme
_____

Weather / Field Conditions
_____

1. Key Highlights / Successes:
-
-
-
-

2. Challenges / Improvement Areas:
-
-
-
-

3. Player Observations:

Player Name	Strengths Shown	Areas to Improve	Notes

4. Team Dynamics & Energy Notes:

(Open reflections on morale, communication, leadership moments, etc.)

5. Adjustments for Next Game:

(Strategies, drills to repeat or tweak, lineup ideas, etc.)

6. Reflection Prompt:

- What did we learn today as a coach and as a team?
- Which players demonstrated growth or leadership today?
- What's one thing we can celebrate before next practice?

PLAY NOTES SHEET
COACHING REFLECTIONS

GAME / PRACTICE DATE _____
OPPONENT / FOCUS THEME _____
WEATHER / FIELD CONDITIONS _____

1. KEY HIGHLIGHTS / SUCCESSES
- _____
- _____

2. CHALLENGES / IMPROVEMENT AREAS
- _____
- _____

3. PLAYER OBSERVATIONS

PLAYER NAME	STRENGTHS SHOWN	AREAS TO IMPROVE	NOTES

4. TEAM DYNAMICS & ENERGY NOTES

5. ADJUSTMENTS FOR NEXT GAME
- What did we learn today as a coach and as as a-team?
- Which players demonstrated growth or leadership today?
- What's one thing we cah celebrate before next practice?

Coaching Journal Template

Encourage coaches to print this sheet weekly, or keep a digital folder (e.g., Canva/Google Sheets version) so that each reflection builds a season-long "Coaching Journal." At the end of the season, these notes become gold for evaluating progress and planning for the next year.

Then, on a side note, you can add a QR code at the bottom of each printable that links to your online play library or demo video.

So ultimately, with digital diagrams and visual playbooks, the game becomes easier to understand. When players can see it, trace it, and recreate it, they don't just memorize plays; they *own* them. This visual foundation makes the transition to game day faster, smoother, and a lot more fun.

SEASON-LONG SKILL PROGRESSION MAPS BY AGE GROUP

Skill development in youth flag football is all about building layers—repetition, understanding, and confidence. A well-structured progression map gives coaches a clear path for gradual improvement while keeping every player motivated. The following roadmap outlines age-specific growth milestones, designed for 10-week seasons (which can be adjusted as needed). Each map focuses on five pillars of development: Flag Pulling, Passing, Catching, Defensive Awareness, and Teamwork.

Ages 6-8: Foundational Learning (Weeks 1-10)

At this stage, the focus is on engagement, enthusiasm, and mastering the basics through play. The goal is to make football feel fun and achievable.

Week	Flag Pulling	Passing	Catching	Defensive Awareness	Teamwork / Attitude
1	Introduce safe flag pulling; practice reaching and grabbing gently.	Basic stance: holding the ball properly.	Catch with both hands, soft toss drills.	Learn "stay in front" concept.	Team introductions, fun names, basic huddle rules.
2	Pull from a stationary partner; no tackling, focus on control.	Throw short underhand tosses.	Soft catches from 2–3 yards.	Understand personal space in defense.	Practice high-fives after plays.
3	Begin chase-and-pull mini games.	One-handed underhand toss with a step forward.	Catch small foam balls while moving.	Introduce "zone" concept: each player covers their area.	Encourage cheering for teammates.
4	React to movement — pull flags in motion.	Introduce the overhand throw motion.	Catch slightly higher passes.	Identify the ball carrier during play.	Learn a simple group chant or team slogan.
5	Combine reaction and pursuit drills.	Practice throwing to moving targets.	Practice "ready hands" before every catch.	Begin awareness of sideline and boundaries.	Share turns fairly; team passing circle.
6	Introduce game-like pull drills (1v1 or 2v2).	Short passes during mini scrimmages.	Catch while jogging, focus on follow-through.	Learn to look for open space defensively.	Talk about sportsmanship and fair play.

7	Develop speed and accuracy in pulls.	Consistent spiral focus.	Introduce catching after a short route.	Recognize offensive setups.	Celebrate small wins (good catch, effort).
8	Reaction + direction drills (coach points direction).	Throw at cone targets.	Catch while turning (basic body rotation).	Learn basic defensive communication (call out "mine").	Rotate leadership for huddle chants.
9	Flag relay races; improve quick grabs.	Pass accuracy contests (fun drills).	Catch mid-speed passes.	Maintain defensive spacing under pressure.	Encourage helping new players.
10	Combine all skills in a fun scrimmage.	Consistent short throws.	Reliable hand-eye co-ordination.	Understanding positioning without reminders.	End-of-season team reflection & celebration.

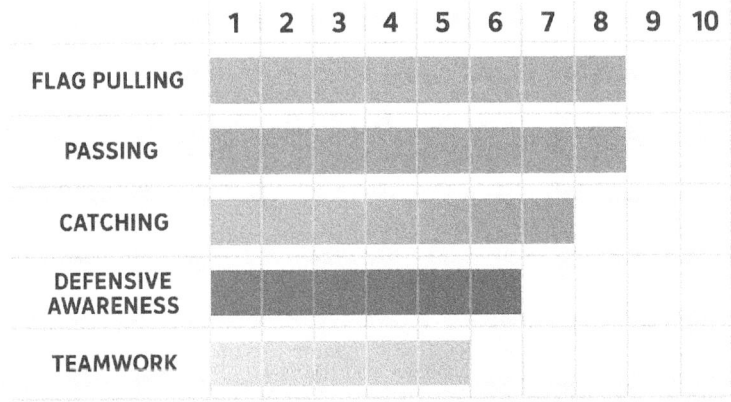

Visual chart or infographic representation of 6–8 Skill Progression Map

Coaching Notes:

- Keep practices light and story-driven. "Capture the Flag" style games work wonders for engagement.
- Reward effort more than skill mastery; at this age, confidence is the goal.
- Reinforce fundamentals visually and verbally every session.
- Encourage parental involvement through weekly progress highlights.

Up next, the roadmap expands for Ages 9–10, where understanding of positions and play patterns begins to take shape, balancing fun with structured learning.

Ages 9–10: Developing Understanding and Control (Weeks 1–10)

This stage bridges fundamentals with understanding. Players begin connecting their individual skills to team strategy, thereby learning why each movement matters. The emphasis here is on precision, awareness, and early decision-making.

Week	Flag Pulling	Passing	Catching	Defensive Awareness	Teamwork / Leadership
1	Review technique from 6–8 level; correct habits.	Reintroduce throwing form, elbow up, step forward.	Review hand positioning; add focus on soft catches.	Relearn defensive stance and zone awareness.	Build trust with teammates through partner drills.

2	Add direction changes mid-run; react quickly.	Introduce leading a receiver (throwing ahead).	Catch while jogging sideways; eyes on the ball.	Communicate during defensive shifts.	Assign small team roles (captain, encourager, setup leader).
3	One-on-one flag pulling with movement variety.	Focus on timing — "throw on three" drills.	Catch from short passes with pressure.	Begin understanding defensive coverage types.	Teach the "talk, move, help" rule during plays.
4	Flag pursuit angles — don't chase straight lines.	Throwing accuracy to stationary targets.	Catch slightly higher passes, mid-chest level.	Recognize fake plays and stay patient.	Begin pre-huddle talk: "What's our plan?"
5	Improve the two-hand pull technique for stability.	Throw under mild defensive pressure.	Catch while backpedaling.	Track opponent eyes and hips for reads.	Celebrate assists, not just touchdowns.
6	Flag tag games with rotation — reaction emphasis.	Passing across the body with balance.	Catching while turning — practice awareness.	Maintain defensive shape while tracking motion.	Lead short chants or timeout resets.
7	Combine pursuit + pull with redirection.	Quick-release throwing (3-second challenge).	Introduce catching routes (slants, quick outs).	Learn to hand off coverage in zones.	Discuss "effort without ego."
8	Flag relay competitions (speed and form).	Throw to moving receivers; aim mid-section.	Catch under mild interference.	Identify offensive spacing; adjust coverage.	Start using positive communication ("Let's fix it!").

| 9 | Defend with awareness — anticipate flag direction. | Refine spiral and control. | Catch with one-hand focus drills (balance practice). | React to offensive formations. | Mentor younger or less confident players. |
| 10 | Game simulation: apply skills in a small-team scrimmage. | Consistent throw form under fatigue. | Catch accurately from varying speeds. | Hold defensive integrity in game flow. | Reflect as a team: what did we master, what's next? |

AGES 9-10 SKILL PROGRESSION MAP

	WEEK 1	WEEK 2	WEEK 3	WEEK 4	WEEK 5	WEEK 6	WEEK 7	WE
FLAG PULLING	STANCE & GRIP	BREAK AWAY	ANGLES	STRIP	STALK	ADVANCED	RECOVERY	CONFI
PASSING	BASIC THROW	QUICK RELEASE	ANKLE HITCH	READ DEFENSE	DECEIVING	VARYING	VERTICAL	TARG
CATCHING	STATIONAR	DRILLS	ONE-HANDED	HIGHBALL	TRAPPING	CONTESTING	SECURING	SECUR
DEFENSIVE AWARENESS	BASIC	EYE CONTACT	ZONES	ANGLE	READ & REACT	POSITIONING	SUPPORT	COVE

Visual Chart or Infographic Representation of Ages 9–10 Skill Progression Map

Coaching Notes:

- Begin integrating simple strategy conversations with kids ("Why did that play work?").
- Encourage controlled intensity—speed with thought.

- Introduce simple leadership principles: taking turns leading stretches, huddles, or cheers.
- Use video or diagram reviews sparingly to start visual learning early.

Then now, we'll raise the bar for **Ages 11–12**, where advanced movement, play understanding, and team-driven execution take center stage.

Ages 11–12: Advanced Execution & Game IQ (Weeks 1–10)

At 11–12, players begin thinking like football players. Physical skills solidify, and cognitive skills—reading covers, creating space, and timing—take center stage. The map below assumes more structured practice time and a willingness to introduce slightly more complex concepts while still keeping it fun and age-appropriate.

Week	Flag Pulling	Passing	Catching	Defensive Awareness	Teamwork / Leadership
1	Review advanced pull mechanics; reinforce two-hand security on strips.	Quarterback footwork and pocket awareness basics.	Catching with contact drill (shield or light obstruction).	Pre-snap reads: identify basic formations.	Assign captains; teach sideline leadership roles.

2	Focus on pursuit angles vs. straight chase; tackle-free containment.	Throwing to rhythm—drop-step, plant, and release.	Catching on the move and over-the-shoulder grabs.	Introduce basic zone responsibilities (3-2 or 2-3 depending on team).	Lead small-group skill breakouts; peer coaching.
3	1v1 competitive pull drills emphasizing technique under fatigue.	Quick game throws, check-downs, and safety valves.	Catching contested balls and securing a second touch.	Man coverage fundamentals: positioning and mirror technique.	Develop pre-play communication (calls, cadence).
4	Strip-and-recover drills (control, not aggression).	Reading defender leverage (throw outside/inside).	High-catch technique and contested jump balls.	Teaching funneling—force plays to help defenders.	Run brief leadership drills; captains lead warm-ups.
5	Reaction + anticipation—reading hips and routes.	Intermediate route combos (slant-flat, shallow-cross).	Catch and transition to run—after-catch vision.	Reading QB eyes and anticipating throws.	Teach mid-game adjustments and simple audibles.
6	Rapid-reaction circuit with fatigue management.	Play-action and fake hand-offs (timing emphasis).	Catching in traffic, quick, secure drills.	Communicate switches and pick up crossers.	Encourage players to give in-play feedback (short, positive).
7	Advanced pursuit scenarios—recover from missed pulls.	Deep ball mechanics: timing, power, and placement.	Route-specific catching (slant, out, curl).	Zone-to-man hybrid concepts; when to switch.	Evaluate and tweak leadership roles; rotate captains.

8	Competitive team flag games with tactical objectives.	Progress reads: primary → secondary → checkdown.	Catch under fatigue; focus on clean reel-in and protect.	Pressure recognition and rush lane awareness.	Players help run short teaching segments for younger groups.
9	Simulated game pressure pulls; situational flag defense.	Two-minute drill basics: clock management and short throws.	Secure catches in scrimmage speed.	Game-sense: alignments vs. offensive motions.	Lead end-of-practice debriefs; set goals for the final week.
10	Full-game simulation with emphasis on execution.	Consistent decision-making under pressure.	Reliable hands across situations; focus on finishing plays.	Maintain discipline in coverage and help with responsibilities.	Season reflection, goal setting for next phase, awards.

AGES 11-12 SKILL PROGRESSION MAP

WEEK	SKILL	
1	Flag Pulling	Passes & Routes
2	Passing	Catching
3	Flag Pulling	Passes & Routes
4	Passing	Catching
5	Defensive Awareness	Flag Pulling
6	Teamwork	Passing
7	Defensive Awareness	Flag Pulling
8	Teamwork	Passing
9	Team'og	Passing
10	Review	Review
11	Rewiew1ro	Game Strategy
12	Somdecor	Game Strategy

Visual Infographic — Ages 11–12 Skill Progression Map

Coaching Notes & Implementation Tips:

- Use short film clips (10–20 seconds) to show correct technique; older kids grasp visual corrections quickly.
- Increase competitive elements gradually and keep the emphasis on technique during competition.
- Begin using simple statistical tracking for core metrics (completed passes, successful flag pulls, catches) to highlight progress.

- When introducing more complex defensive concepts, use color-coded cones or wristbands to simplify roles visually.
- Encourage player-led micro-coaching: asking a player to demonstrate and explain a concept accelerates understanding.

MILESTONES, SKILL CHECKS & COACHING BADGES

Skill development isn't linear; it grows through checkpoints of confidence. By introducing mini skill checks, printable badges, and adaptable progression tips, coaches can track performance while keeping the journey fun and rewarding.

1. Mini Skill-Checks (Every 2–3 Weeks)

Short, structured assessments help players recognize growth and identify areas needing refinement.

Skill Area	Assessment Example	Success Marker	Coaching Focus
Flag Pulling	Timed 1v1 flag drill under movement	Clean pull within 3 seconds	Read angles, stay balanced
Passing	5-throw accuracy challenge	4/5 throws within the target zone	Emphasize mechanics over distance
Catching	Catching 10 passes from varying angles	8/10 clean catches	Eye contact with the ball, soft hands
Defense Awareness	Shadow tag coverage drill	Maintain positioning 80% of the time	Body alignment, anticipation
Teamwork	Cooperative relay or rotation drill	Full participation and communication	Supportive communication, positivity

Announce skill-check weeks ahead of time; kids love working toward "Check Week." It adds excitement and accountability.

2. Assessment Rubrics for Tracking Progress

Use a simple 1–5 rating system to measure each player's progress:

Score	Meaning	Coaching Note
1	Needs strong improvement	Focused drills required; simplify tasks
2	Emerging ability	Reinforce fundamentals through repetition
3	Consistent performance	Ready for the next stage of challenge
4	Strong mastery	Add variation and mild competition
5	Leadership level	Encourage peer coaching and mentorship

Create laminated player cards that allow coaches to quickly jot down weekly notes or add stickers to mark milestones reached.

3. Challenge Badges and Certificates

Reward progress visually. Certificates and badges act as powerful motivators; they recognize effort, not just talent.

Badge Name	Criteria	Reward Idea
● **Flag Pulling Pro**	Achieves 3 consecutive clean flag pulls in a game or scrimmage	Printed badge or iron-on patch
● **Route Running Champ**	Runs assigned routes correctly 90% of the time in drills	Certificate signed by the coach

● **Hands of Steel**	Catches 8/10 passes in skill check	Small wristband or team shoutout
● **Defensive Wall**	Holds zone coverage without leaving position	Sticker or magnet badge
● **Team Spirit Leader**	Demonstrates positive attitude and encouragement	Team "Star of the Week" ribbon

Encourage coaches to let players design their own next badge goal; it fosters ownership and self-drive.

4. Adjusting for Team Pace: Accelerating or Reinforcing

Every team develops differently. Some absorb concepts faster, while others need repetition to solidify basics. Great coaching adapts.

For Fast-Advancing Teams:
- Combine drills (e.g., catching + route running).
- Introduce play variations or add a decision element ("choose route based on defense").
- Rotate leadership tasks and have players explain plays or strategies.

For Teams Needing More Time:
- Simplify drills without removing challenge, shorten distances, or reduce moving parts.
- Focus on confidence first; small wins build momentum.
- Use peer modeling, pair stronger players with developing ones.

For Mixed-Level Teams:

- Divide groups by challenge level but rotate frequently so no one feels isolated.
- Create "progression tiers" (Bronze, Silver, Gold) for each core skill.

Track weekly team "focus themes"—like "Ball Security Week" or "Communication Week" to unify attention while customizing pace for different skill groups.

5. Revisiting Fundamentals Without Losing Engagement

Repetition doesn't have to feel repetitive. Coaches can make refreshers fun:

- Turn drills into games (e.g., flag relay races, catching challenges).
- Introduce time or accuracy scoring for repetition drills.
- Add "Beat the Coach" mini-competitions.
- Use variety in the environment, rotate field areas or drill directions.

Tip: Revisit fundamentals as refinement*,* not review*.* Phrase it as: "Let's level up our basics," so it feels like progress, not repetition.

Through consistent milestones, engaging challenges, and adaptable pacing, young athletes don't just grow in skill, they grow in confidence, awareness, and teamwork. That's the real win of every great youth flag football season.

TROUBLESHOOTING AND TRIUMPH

Every coach has been in a situation when only half the team shows up, the drills fall apart, a parent complains, or a kid loses heart after a fumble. It's part of the game. But it's also where the best coaching happens in how we respond when things don't go as planned. Sometimes, what you're really coaching isn't football. It's confidence, communication, and calm under pressure. The following are what real coaches learn on the field, in the heat of frustration, laughter, and breakthrough.

Low Attendance

When only four kids show up, don't cancel, adjust. Turn it into an intimate skills clinic or small-team challenge. Let the kids who came feel special for being there. Reward effort, not turnout. Text parents later with highlights, not guilt trips. Enthusiasm spreads faster than reminders.

"We ran a three-player passing circuit. They loved the attention. Next week? Full turnout."

When the Skill Gap Widens

Some kids are naturals while others need time. Mix and rotate groups so no one feels left behind or bored. Let advanced players lead short demos because this gives them a sense of pride, whilst also teaching them patience. The key is to make every drill scalable: faster for some, slower for others, but always fun.

"Our strongest rusher became our teaching captain. The shy kids started following his lead. That day, we built a team."

When the Sideline Turns Loud

Parents mean well, but sometimes passion spills over. Have a quick pre-season talk about sideline conduct. Keep one printed parent agreement handy. If things heat up mid-game, call for a timeout, not a confrontation. A calm tone defuses chaos faster than authority.

"We didn't argue. I asked her to join the post-game water duty. She saw how much work went in—problem solved."

When Players Lose Heart

After a dropped pass or missed flag, emotions can sink fast. Bend down, meet them eye level, and remind them: *'Mistakes are proof we're trying.'* Let the team clap for effort, not just success. Build resilience as deliberately as you build routes.

"He dropped every pass that day. But when the team cheered him on, he caught the next one. That moment changed him."

When Chaos Tests You

Sometimes you'll lose control of practice. Balls flying, kids laughing, plan gone. Take a breath, smile, and regain rhythm with something familiar, such as a team chant, a simple game, or a water break. The goal isn't to control energy but to redirect it.

"I realized the noise meant joy. We channeled it into relay races—best session all season."

When You Need Quick Fixes

- **If only 4 kids show up:** Play 2v2 scrimmages, focus on repetition, or rotate through skill stations.

- **If equipment is missing:** Improvise with cones, shoes, or imagination; creativity is half the fun.
- **If tempers flare:** Pull players aside quietly; use calm voices and empathy over punishment.

Youth flag football shapes character throughout the entire learning process. Every missed catch, every unexpected win, every solved sideline challenge is another page in your coaching story. You're not just teaching football; you're teaching how to get back up.

And that, coach, is the victory that lasts far beyond the season whistle.

CONCLUSION:
UNDER THE LIGHTS

The field is quiet now. The sun has dropped low, turning the last cones into silhouettes. You can still hear the echo of laughter from earlier: the chase for a flag, the cheer after a catch, the coach's whistle cutting through the wind.

The drills are done.

The plans are drawn.

The season, or the first one, is about to begin.

This moment is where the real work starts. You've read through the pages. You've learned how to build a team from scratch, how to teach, how to organize, how to handle chaos with grace. You've seen how flag football isn't just a sport but a classroom, a playground, and a mirror for life. You now carry everything you need: the rules, the drills, the plays, the structure. But more than that, you carry understanding. You know the why behind every flag pulled and every high-five shared.

Remember, youth flag football was never about trophies or statistics. It's about the courage to show up, the humility

CONCLUSION:
UNDER THE LIGHTS

The field is quiet now. The sun has dropped low, turning the last cones into silhouettes. You can still hear the echo of laughter from earlier: the chase for a flag, the cheer after a catch, the coach's whistle cutting through the wind.

The drills are done.

The plans are drawn.

The season, or the first one, is about to begin.

This moment is where the real work starts. You've read through the pages. You've learned how to build a team from scratch, how to teach, how to organize, how to handle chaos with grace. You've seen how flag football isn't just a sport but a classroom, a playground, and a mirror for life. You now carry everything you need: the rules, the drills, the plays, the structure. But more than that, you carry understanding. You know the why behind every flag pulled and every high-five shared.

Remember, youth flag football was never about trophies or statistics. It's about the courage to show up, the humility to learn, and the joy of seeing others grow. It's about watching a kid who once hid behind teammates now calling a play with confidence. It's about parents cheering louder for effort than for touchdowns. It's about communities finding connection one Saturday morning at a time.

That's what this handbook was written for: to empower you to build something that lasts longer than a season.

So whether you're a parent holding the playbook, a coach tying your whistle, or a young player lacing up your sneakers, remember this: what you've learned here isn't meant to stay on paper. It's meant to live on the field.

When you step onto that grass, you're not just starting practice; you're continuing a story that began long before you. You're part of a tradition that values inclusion over intimidation, growth over glory, and laughter over perfection. You're shaping the next generation, not just of athletes, but of teammates, leaders, and friends.

So take a breath. Let the field call to you. Feel the quiet before the first whistle. That's the sound of potential waiting.

Go ahead and set up the cones. Gather the kids. Look across the field and know that every inch of it is now yours to fill with learning, laughter, and leadership.

The playbook ends here, but the season begins now.

This is your field. Your team. Your moment.

Drills are over.

Game on.

REFERENCES

- *Beginner's Guide to Flag Football.* (n.d.). Gridiron Football. https://gridironfb.com/blogs/news/how-to-play-flag-football
- Broun, H. (2015, April 8). *Sports do not build character; They Reveal It.* Quoteinvestigator.com. https://quoteinvestigator.com/2015/04/08/sports/
- Chapman, C. (n.d.). *Movement skills for children.* Ukcoaching.org. https://www.ukcoaching.org/ukc-club/resources/movement-skills-for-children/
- Dawg, A. (2024, September 26). *The history of flag football.* Alphadawgflagfootball. https://alphadawgflagfootball.com/youth-flag-football/the-history-of-flag-football/
- *Developing physically active and sporty kids - benefits and barriers.* (2019a). Physiopedia. https://www.physio-pedia.com/Developing_Physically_Active_and_Sporty_Kids_-_Benefits_and_Barriers
- *Developing physically active and sporty kids - benefits and barriers.* (2019b). Physiopedia. https://www.physio-pedia.com/

- Developing_Physically_Active_and_Sporty_Kids_-_Benefits_and_Barriers
- Gridiron Team. (n.d.-a). *Beginner's guide to flag football.* Gridiron Football. https://gridironfb.com/blogs/news/how-to-play-flag-football
- Gridiron Team. (n.d.-b). *The unlikely origins of flag football.* Gridiron Football. https://gridironfb.com/blogs/news/the-unlikely-origins-of-flag-football
- *How to Play Flag Football | NFL FLAG.* (n.d.). Nflflag. https://nflflag.com/coaches/flag-football-rules/how-to-play-flag-football
- International Olympic Committee. (n.d.-a). *Flag Football: Olympic history, rules, latest updates and upcoming events for the Olympic sport.* Olympics.com. https://www.olympics.com/en/sports/flag-football/
- International Olympic Committee. (n.d.-b). *Flag Football: Olympic history, rules, latest updates and upcoming events for the Olympic sport.* Olympics. https://www.olympics.com/en/sports/flag-football/
- Little Lifters. (n.d.). *The science of motor skill development: Why early movement matters.* Little Lifters. Retrieved October 28, 2025, from https://www.littlelifters.co.uk/blogs/little-lifters-blog/the-science-of-motor-skill-development-why-early-movement-matters?srsltid=AfmBOoqb3Wuwbkym88UstZ8eCg8Wldbv-IvaJfRH9m8VtYWVtB4eOI-d

- Ljubljana Frogs. (2021, October). *History of flag football.* Ljubljanafrogs.si. https://ljubljanafrogs.si/en/posts/the-history-of-flag-football
- Lombardi, V. (n.d.). *The will to win is not nearly so important as the will to prepare to win.* PrimeGenesis. https://www.primegenesis.com/our-blog/2010/11/popularity-of-lombardi-will-to-prepare-to-win-post/
- Paterno, J. (n.d.). *The will to win is important, but the will to prepare is vital.* BrainyQuote. Retrieved November 10, 2025, from https://www.brainyquote.com/quotes/joe_paterno_125242
- Roosevelt, T. (n.d.). *People don't care how much you know until they know how much you care.* Goodreads.com. https://www.goodreads.com/quotes/34690-people-don-t-care-how-much-you-know-until-they-know
- Soule, K. (n.d.). *The unlikely origins of flag football.* Gridiron Football. https://gridironfb.com/blogs/news/the-unlikely-origins-of-flag-football
- Swigert, S. (2018, June 29). *How to start a flag football league.* Jerseywatch.com; Jersey Watch. https://www.jerseywatch.com/blog/how-to-start-a-flag-football-league
- Wooden, J. (2019). *It's the little details that are vital. Little things make big things happen.* BrainyQuote; BrainyQuote. https://www.brainyquote.com/quotes/john_wooden_384652
- *Youth Flag Football Programs & Leagues at i9 Sports®.* (n.d.). I9 Sports. https://www.i9sports.com/flag-football

www.ingramcontent.com/pod-product-compliance
Lightning Source LLC
Chambersburg PA
CBHW070328010526
44107CB00004B/459